Western Isles Discovery Book

Alison Johnson

with illustrations by Bill Neill

Contents

1. In with a splash!

No, it's not an albatross. It's a gannet with a white head and dark wings – that means it's a young one.

The Western Isles are WAY OUT! Look on the map – there's a lot of sea to cross from Scotland. If you live in the islands anyway, chances are you see the sea every day – maybe all day! When you go on the ferry, you're probably thinking about the shops in Inverness or Glasgow. But for most visitors to the islands, the sea itself is NEWS...

If you're a visitor, and live in Glasgow or Wyre Piddle or Salt Lake City, a gannet is just about as rare as an albatross anyway. So, don't take gannets for granted, living with gannets is special. Next time you go on the ferry, or out fishing with Dad, LOOK!

...or LISTEN!
If you arrive by air rather than sea, the first bird you hear may be one of the rarest! Corncrakes breed in the long grass near the airstrips. For more about corncrakes, see p.27.

Gannets are our largest seabird. First year birds start dark all over. Adult birds (from about 4 years old) are pure white except for black wingtips and butter-yellow head, with grey-blue beak and legs. Their bodies are shaped very like Concorde to zoom powerfully through the air without causing turbulence. Their wings are long and narrow (2 metre wingspan) for the same reason. They fly in well-disciplined groups, in lines or vee formations – and then they *dive*! A gannet's dive is a wonder of the the bird world, perpendicularly down for maybe 30m into the sea after fish. A human hitting the water at that speed would probably be killed, but the gannet's collar-bones are honeycombed with air-spaces, which absorb the shock of these dives. Gannets spend most of their lives at sea, only coming to land to breed, in huge crowded colonies on remote islands. The gannets you see off the Western Isles breed on St Kilda or Sula Sgeir – sulaire is Gaelic for gannet.

whale watch

Cetaceans (whales and dolphins) are sea mammals, breathing air as we do, but capable of long, deep dives between breaths. You can count yourself very lucky if you see them, but the ferries are great lookouts, so now's your chance! Clifftops like Barra Head and Tiumpan Head are also good. Calm days are best for whale-spotting. A crowd of diving seabirds sometimes gives a clue – they may be after a share of the leavings.

There are identification charts on the ferries – look out for them.

Cetaceans divide into toothed whales and baleen whales. Baleen whales feed by sieving mouthfuls of sea water – quite a mouthful in the case of a great whale! – through fringed bony plates (baleen) in their throats, to extract tiny sea-creatures from the water. Baleen was the 'whalebone' in Great-Grandmama's corsets.

'Ceta' means fat – so cetaceans are fatties! Since they are warm-blooded, unlike most creatures that spend their lives in cold water, they have a thick layer of fat to keep them warm. This fat is called blubber, and it was mainly for the oil obtained from blubber that whales were hunted. Whales used to be a welcome source of flesh, oil, bone and baleen to island communities. Look on the map for placenames containing the Gaelic word muc, which means a pig, usually a 'sea-pig', or whale. This was very small scale hunting though.

Porpoises are our smallest and most common cetaceans – 1.4 -1.8m. Very dark.

Not all phins belong to dolphins...You may be looking at a **basking shark**. These huge creatures can grow up to 9 metres – 4 – 5 metres is usual. If the fin you are watching cruises along the surface rather than rolling, and if you can see two other black bits wiggling fore and aft of the fin that aren't quite like anything you've ever seen before, you are probably looking at a basking shark. If one comes alongside when you are in a boat, you may be lucky enough to get a good look into its huge, gaping jaws – not a tooth in sight! This shark won't bite you. The basking shark feeds on tiny plankton sieved through its gills from the seawater. It cruises along just below the surface, with not only its dorsal fin, but the tip of its nose and the point of its tail above the water. Basking sharks used to be very common round the west coast of Scotland, but they have been badly hit by fishing, some of it for oil, some for 'sport'.

Last century whaling became a very profitable business. That was why many whale species were driven almost to extinction. At Buonavoneader in Harris are the remains of an old whaling station.

Perhaps one of the most hopeful developments for whales is whale-watching tourism, which can bring as good profits as killing the animals. However, if you are ever lucky enough to watch whales or dolphins this way, don't chase them or otherwise annoy them. It may be great fun for us to get close enough to touch, but it can be very bad for the whales, who need to be left to feed, rest and look after their young in peace.

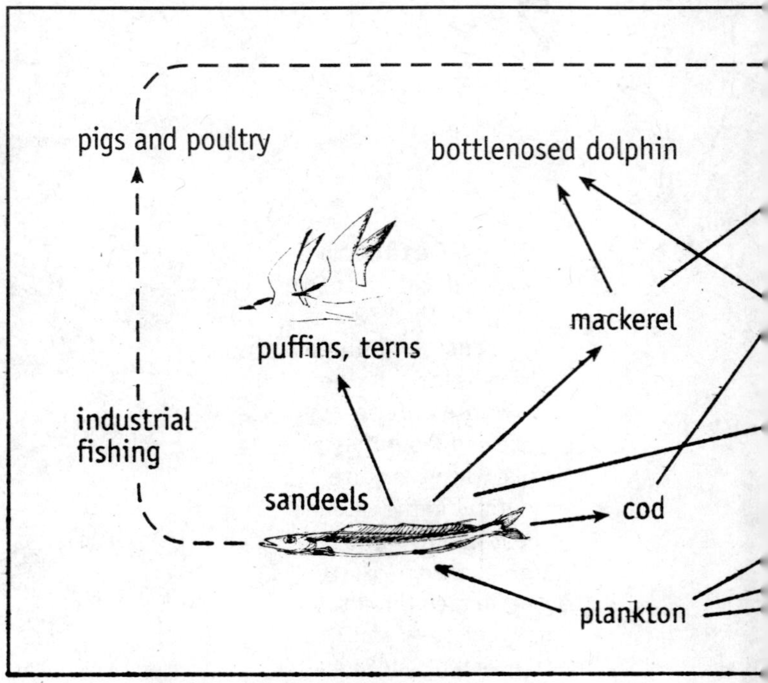

who eats who?

<u>Predators</u> are creatures that get their food by hunting others as <u>prey</u>. The <u>food web</u> shows examples of who eats who. A <u>top predator</u> is one which doesn't get eaten itself. Seals are pretty much top predators – unless, that is, killer whales move into the neighbourhood...

Seals are often blamed for taking fish. Seal numbers are high because they are no longer hunted by humans around Europe, and yes, they do eat fish! However, it is not at all certain that less seals means more fish of the sorts <u>we</u> like to eat, because many of the fish taken by seals themselves prey on the young of the very sorts we <u>do</u> like. In Canada, where seals have been blamed for collapse of cod fisheries, and where people consequently kill thousands of seals, there is no sign of the cod coming back.

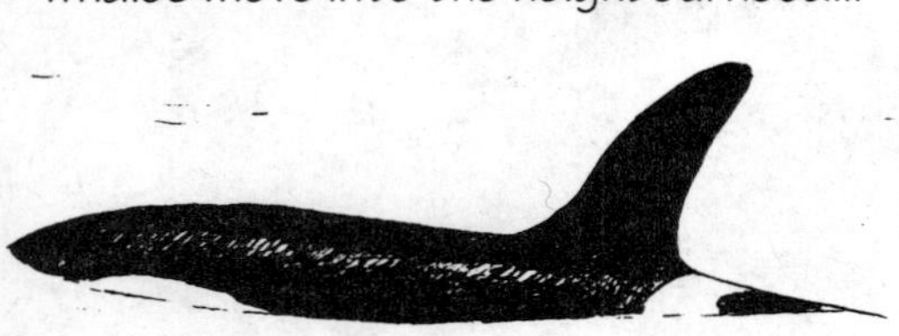

killer whale 4 – 8m. Black with white spot behind very tall fin. Fast!

pilot whale 4.8 – 8.5m. Almost black with white throat. Very long (not tall) fin. Surfaces at 1 – 2 minute intervals

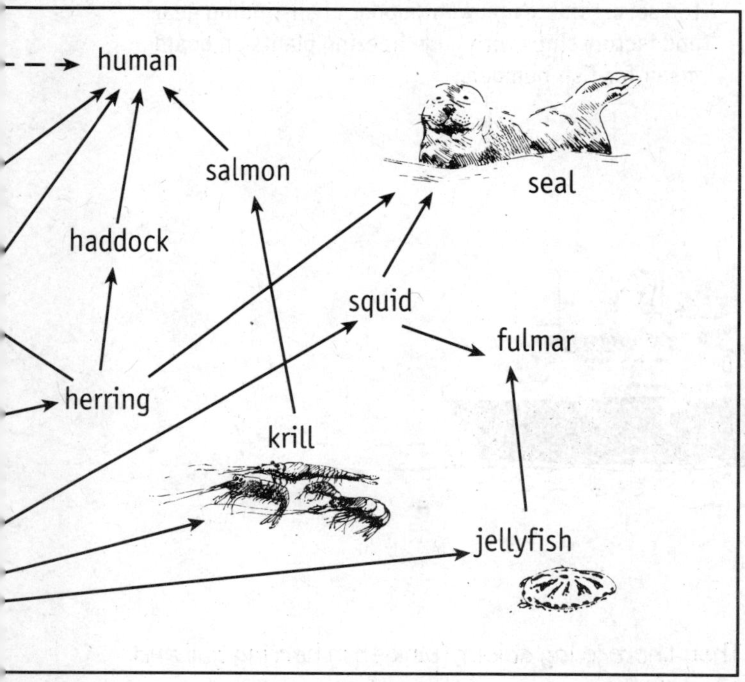

There are two types of seal round British coasts – grey seals and common seals.

Grey seals Large. Silvery grey with dark spots on the back and head. They are actually a rare species in world terms, but a third of them live around the Western Isles, so you will be pretty sure of seeing them here. Look out for them even in Stornoway harbour! In the water, they're friendly and curious towards humans. But they need remote islands or beaches away from human interference to breed, because they are clumsy

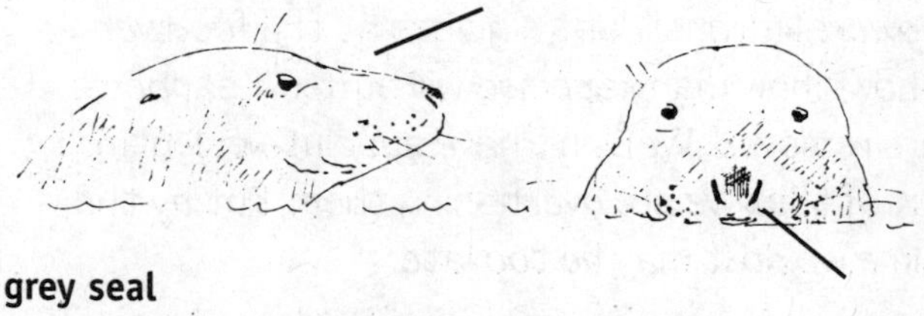

grey seal

For quick identification, look at the nose.

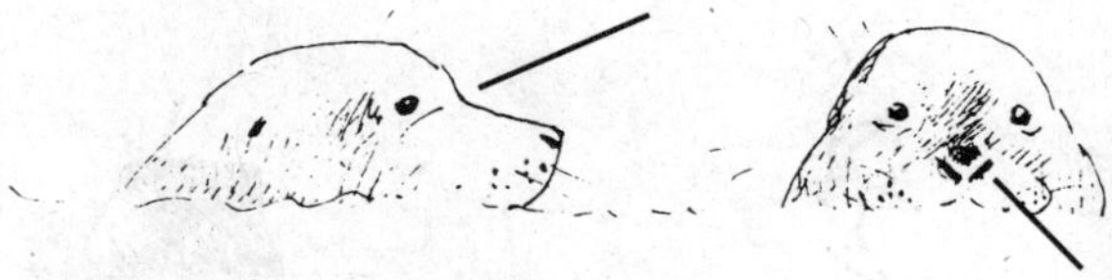

common seal

and slow on land. The pups are born in autumn, and fed on very rich milk for about two weeks. Then the females mate with the resident bull and go back to sea leaving the pups, which have trebled in weight, to fend for themselves. Only the strongest mature males breed, as they have to guard a territory with a 'harem' of females from other males. This is so exhausting that females live two or three times as long as males.15 is old for a bull seal but a cow can live to be 40.

Common seals are smaller. Their fur can be any colour of fawn or brown, with darker spots all over. They prefer sheltered inshore waters. The pups are born in summer, on a rocky skerry or sandbank, and can swim at once. They stay with their mothers for two or three months. You may be lucky enough to see one hitching a lift on Mum's back as she swims along.

Risso's dolphin 3 – 4.2m. Light grey with fine white lines. Tall curved fin.

minke whale 8 – 10.2m. Dark bluish grey. Small pointed fin set very far back. Surfaces at 40 – 50 second intervals.

One of the big unknowns in fishing is the **sandeel**.

This tiny, silvery fish, as you can see from the foodweb, is eaten by large numbers of other species, and is particularly valuable food for the young of seabirds and for many species of larger fish which we like to eat. Sandeels are fished by humans in large quantities – not because we eat them, but to make meal for farmed salmon or poultry, for fertiliser, and even to fuel powerstations! Just a glance at the foodweb shows how many species will suffer if sandeels are removed. We don't have absolute scientific proof that we are overfishing them, but by the time we do it may be too late.

Predators, even top ones, rarely eat themselves out of house and home. In the natural world, if one generation eats too many fish dinners, the next generation will starve, and prey numbers will recover. Or if prey numbers go down, opportunistic species (like the fulmar or herring gull) may eat something else which is plentiful for a while. Unfortunately, we humans can, and do, take far more fish than we need for food even though it is often wasted, and we don't tend to worry about wiping out prey species, because we can always eat something else instead. But if there is going to be food left in the oceans for us, let alone for all the other creatures that depend on the sea, we should be worrying – and doing something about it. Our technology has been too successful: think what modern fish-finding gear and factory ships with huge freezing plants on board mean for fish numbers.

You may not see whales from the boat, but you'll always see something interesting! Even if it's only gulls. Only gulls? Did you know you might see six different types from the ferry?

The most difficult to separate are the herring gull and common gull. If they are together, size helps.

Then there is leg colour (pinkish in herring gull and greenish in common gull), and look out for the common gull's black eye!

The different position of the eye in the face of the common gull makes it look friendlier than the herring gull. But don't be fooled by that, it's no angel either, at least not if you are a wader chick!

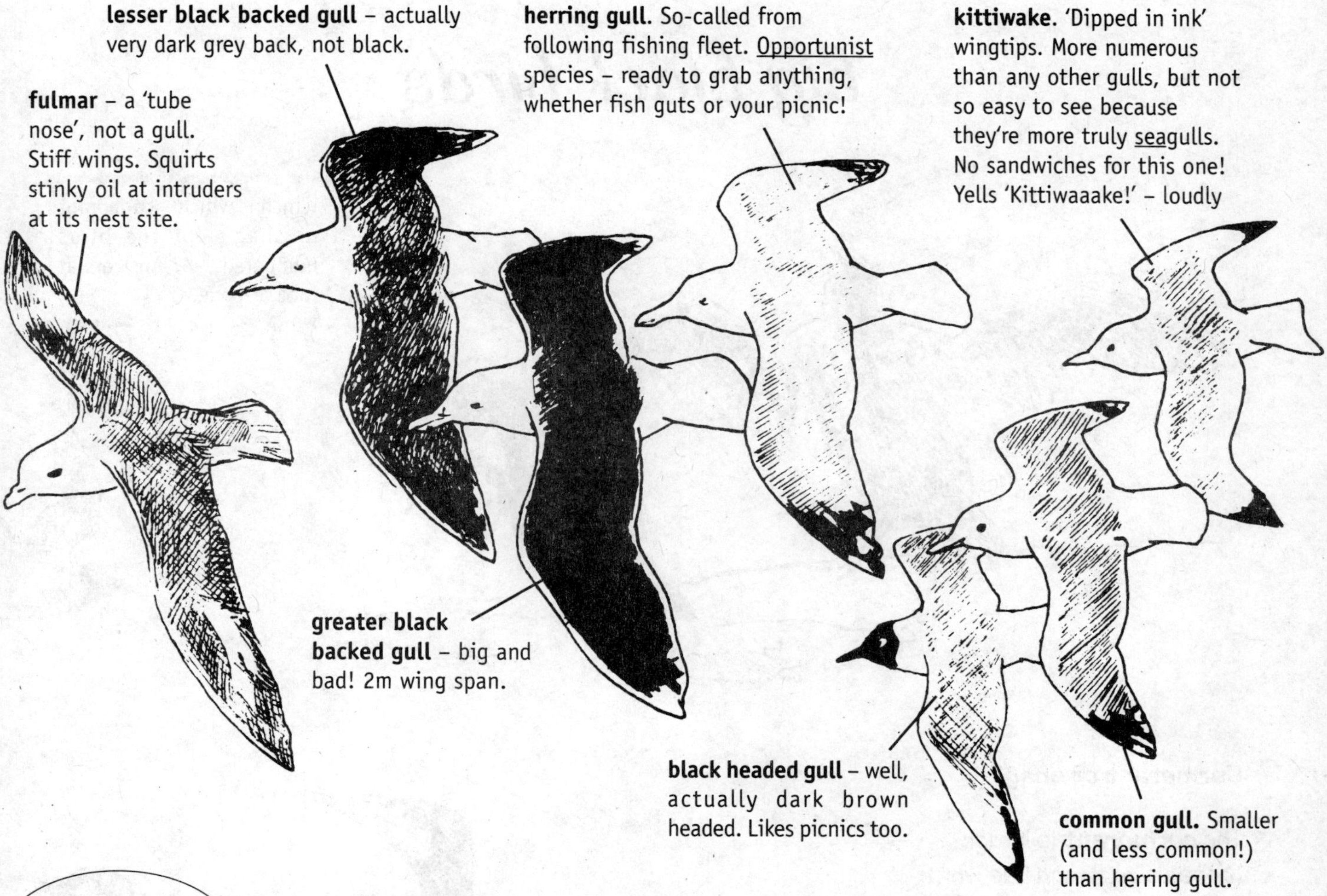

What is the largest British gull?

Which three species have misleading names?

Which gull shouts its own name?

Herring and black backed gulls have a red spot on the side of their bills. Chicks peck at the spot when they want their parents to cough up the food they have brought.

Gull chicks hatch in May. They are mottly brown for the next two years, except kittiwake.

big black birds

Which is which – cormorant or shag – of the birds numbered 1-4? Answers at foot of page.

Cormorant or shag?

The **cormorant** is larger (goose sized), and has white cheeks. The **shag** (duck sized) has a metallic green gloss, and a crest in the breeding season. Both swim with bodies low in the water, diving in a half somersault, showing their feet (unlike the various seaducks and divers, which go smoothly down with no fuss). Both cormorants and shags often stand with wings spread out, probably to help fish they've swallowed to slide down their gullets! The young of both birds are dull brown, cormorants paler underneath.

1 cormorant (white cheeks)
2 shag (not breeding, no crest)
3 shag (breeding, crested)
4 cormorant (white cheeks)

black and white

There are NO purple or orange seabirds! Probably the nearest thing you'll find is the puffin's beak – and you may actually find it on the beach, because after the breeding season the birds shed their splendid blue, red and yellow beak covers.

The **puffin** is one of the **auks,** bustling little black and white seabirds. On most ferry crossings you will see auks whirring to and fro or bobbing around on the waves. Notice that when they're startled, they're just as likely to dive as fly off, and if you are watching from a small boat, you'll see they carry on flying under water! All auk species dive for small fish, but at different levels, so that they don't compete with each other for food. Because they swim so fast under water, auks, especially guillemots which dive deeply, are among the most common accidental victims of fishing nets.

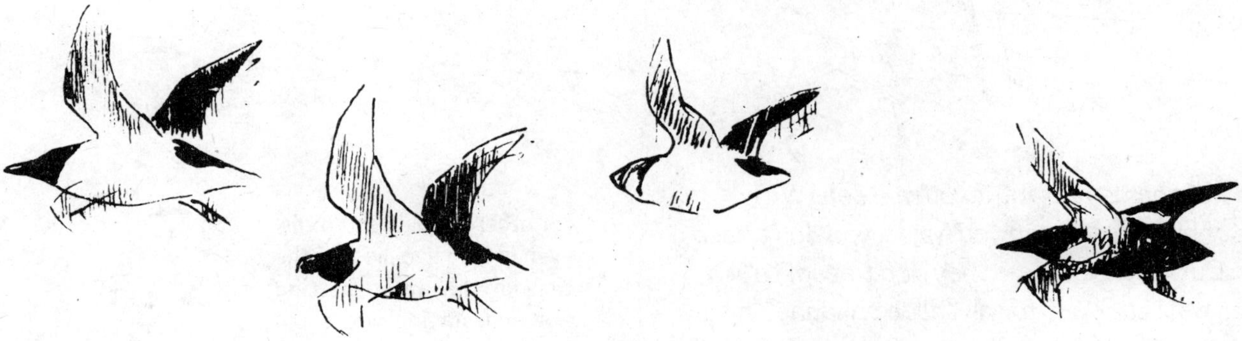

The Shiant Islands are a famous seabird haunt, which you can see in the distance from the ferries to Lewis and Harris. The name 'shiant' means 'blessed' or 'enchanted'. Maybe they got their name from the eerie songs of seabirds and seals echoing back from the steep cliffs. When you are level with the Shiants on the ferry, keep your binoculars busy – it's your best chance of seeing puffins in the area, as they fly busily to and from their nests there all summer.

When puffin parents leave the colony in mid August, the chicks have to make their own way to sea. They do this at night, to avoid hungry black-backed gulls. Young puffins are drawn to glimmering light – which should naturally be the sea, reflecting stars or moon. But where puffins nest anywhere near streetlights, they head for these instead! 'Puffin patrols' at the army base on St Kilda put the bewildered puffins in boxes till dawn, then release them out to sea.

guillemot

puffin greyish cheeks, THE BEAK, fine pair of orange feet.

razorbill stout bill for catching the slightly larger fish they prefer.

black guillemot (**tystie**) very dark grey, white bars on the wings, magnificent bright scarlet feet.

stormy weather

The seas around the Western Isles are rich in life and warmer than you might expect so far north, because of the **North Atlantic Drift** flowing from the warm Gulf of Mexico. Without this current, northern Scotland would be much colder – although we might not get so much rain! Rain is caused when moist air from the sea meets high ground – which may be colder in winter than the sea, and warmer in summer. The difference in temperature causes condensation (rain or mist). The island hills are the first land Atlantic weather systems meet for thousands of miles so there is a long way for wind and waves to build up.

Island weather is all right if you're a seal! With 20cm of blubber to keep you warm, you don't need a mac. But all the same – they don't seem to like getting wet! Look out for all these bananas on the rocks when the tide is coming in. They're seals – resting on their tummies, with their heads and hind flippers stuck as far out of the water as possible.

Seals love to bask – that is, to haul out on a rock, if possible in the sunshine, to snooze and dry off (sometimes they snore). Once their fur is warm and dry, getting back in the cold water is probably a bit of a shock, just as it is for us when we've been sunbathing. But because of their thick blubber, they can stay in indefinitely without their insides cooling down.

As for us humans – better not forget that anorak! There are lots of things to look for outdoors in the islands – but be prepared for the Atlantic weather. Wind and dampness can make you feel much colder. Wellies are a must, and carry a warm garment and a waterproof one in a backpack for emergencies.

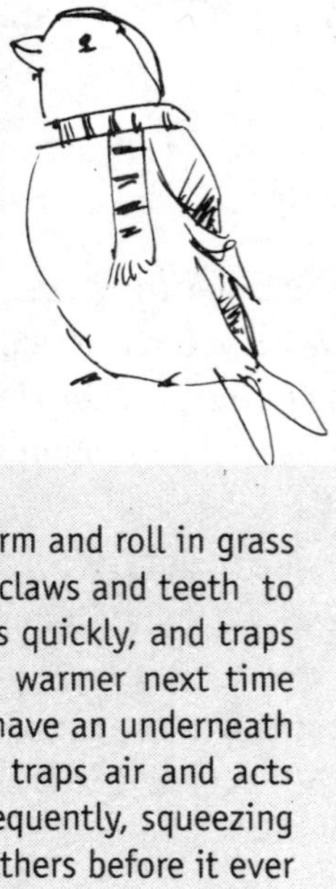

For other animals and birds, even if they live most of the time in the water, getting wet and staying wet could dangerously lower their body temperature. Different species cope in different ways. **Otters** wash in fresh water if they have been in the sea, because salt remaining in their fur would attract moisture. Then they squirm and roll in grass or heather, and finally they use claws and teeth to comb out the fur so that it dries quickly, and traps some air which will keep them warmer next time they enter the water. **Seabirds** have an underneath layer of downy feathers, which traps air and acts like a down quilt. They preen frequently, squeezing water out of the top layer of feathers before it ever penetrates to the down, and with a powdery substance from the preen gland under the tail, they carefully arrange each feather, so that they overlap closely and shed water – rather like a slated roof, but much more complicated. If you watch sea-ducks, you may notice them preening even while they are bobbing around in the waves.

Now we're ready to take a walk through the islands, starting on a great sand beach, or in Gaelic, traigh mhòr.

keep it on file

Wind and waves and the rain they bring made the Hebrides what they are today – surfy sandy beaches on the west, bare rugged mountains separating Lewis from Harris, hundreds of freshwater lochs in the Uists, the low-lying brown peatlands of Lewis. All these are different habitats.

Habitat means somewhere to live, and different sorts of places attract different residents.

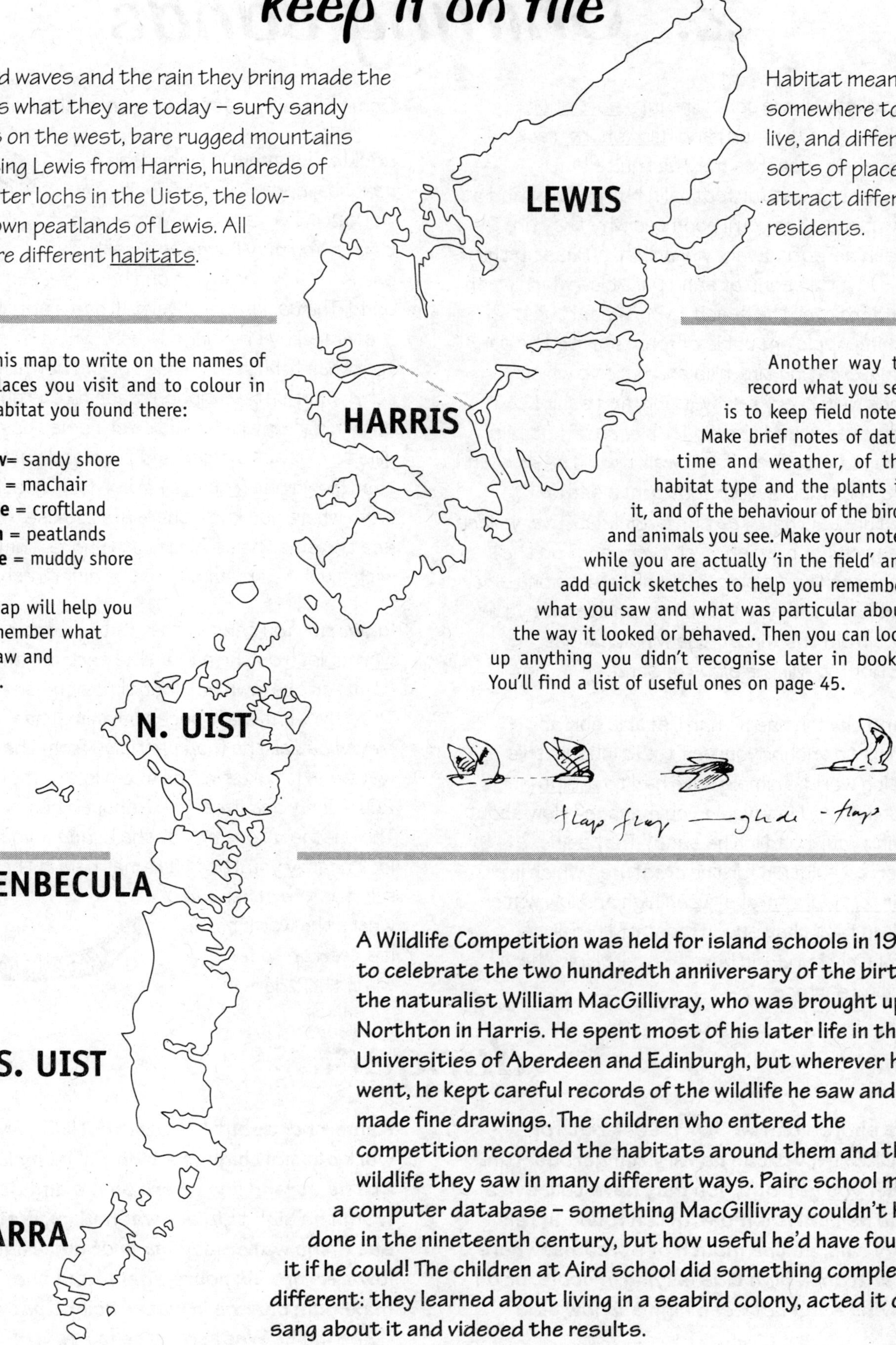

Use this map to write on the names of the places you visit and to colour in the habitat you found there:

yellow= sandy shore
green = machair
orange = croftland
brown = peatlands
purple = muddy shore

The map will help you to remember what you saw and where.

Another way to record what you see is to keep field notes. Make brief notes of date, time and weather, of the habitat type and the plants in it, and of the behaviour of the birds and animals you see. Make your notes while you are actually 'in the field' and add quick sketches to help you remember what you saw and what was particular about the way it looked or behaved. Then you can look up anything you didn't recognise later in books. You'll find a list of useful ones on page 45.

A Wildlife Competition was held for island schools in 1996 to celebrate the two hundredth anniversary of the birth of the naturalist William MacGillivray, who was brought up at Northton in Harris. He spent most of his later life in the Universities of Aberdeen and Edinburgh, but wherever he went, he kept careful records of the wildlife he saw and made fine drawings. The children who entered the competition recorded the habitats around them and the wildlife they saw in many different ways. Pairc school made a computer database – something MacGillivray couldn't have done in the nineteenth century, but how useful he'd have found it if he could! The children at Aird school did something completely different: they learned about living in a seabird colony, acted it out, sang about it and videoed the results.

Scattered through this book you'll find out what the other children did to record the wildlife habitats around them. You might like to use some of their ideas.

2. Shifting sands

Naturalists divide coastline into soft shore (pebbles, sand or mud) and hard shore (rock). Some sandy beaches may feel quite hard underfoot (great for football!) but if you stand at the water's edge you'll soon see why they are classed as 'soft'. Every wave that surges up the beach is a thin soup of sand particles which wash to and fro over the beach. Even the farthest-reaching ripple or bubble of foam starts the sand moving, creating tiny hills and hollows which change with every new wetting, and sculpt themselves round the bigger pieces of flotsam and round your feet. If you walk up to the dry sand above the tideline, your footprints set up miniature earthquakes and landslides. Every piece of seaweed or rubbish, even every shell on the upper beach has a sloping hill of sand to one side of it: that's the side which was sheltered by the object from the wind. If the wind changes direction, so will the slope of sand.

A sandy beach has no hard, stable surface – nothing to anchor yourself to. To inhabit this shifting world, animals have had to adapt in special ways. How would you manage? How about burying your head in the sand? That's the preferred solution for the creatures which live in the intertidal zone, between high and low water mark. In fact they spend most of their lives completely buried, in burrows well below the churning surface.

Some of the easiest-to-see intertidal animals are:

cockle. Common on Hebridean beaches, especially the Cockle Strand in Barra and Luskentyre in Harris. You may have seen just shells, or a live one lying on the surface of the sand. The cockle is a bivalve. It has a soft body protected by two hinged shells which fit exactly together. It buries itself 2 – 10cm down in the sand, with just its siphon reaching the surface to suck in water, which is filtered inside the animal's gills to extract oxygen and tiny food particles, then blown out (exhaled). If you look closely at wet sand where you know there are cockles, you will see the small holes for their siphons, sometimes with a bubble appearing as the animal exhales.

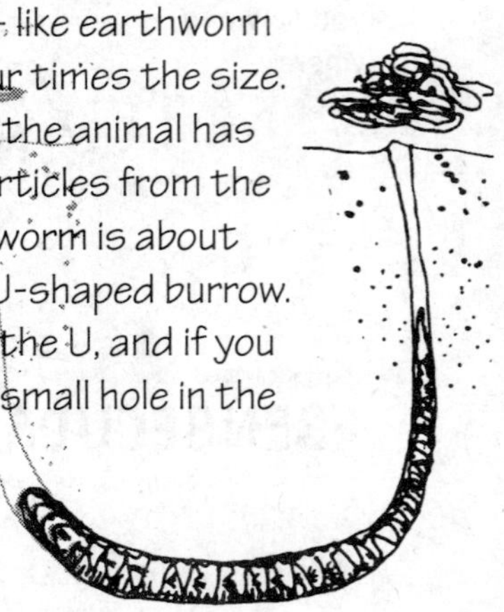

lugworm. You can tell they're there from the wormcasts on the sand – like earthworm casts on the lawn but four times the size. They are what's left once the animal has sieved out all the food particles from the wet sand it takes in. The worm is about 20cm long, and lives in a U-shaped burrow. The cast is at one end of the U, and if you look nearby you'll see the small hole in the sand at the other end, where the worm pokes its head up to feed when the tide is in.

danger!

Soft shores can be SOFT! Look out for QUICKSAND. It can be very dangerous – and even if you get out, you may have to leave a wellie behind! It's most often found after heavy rain, at the mouth of streams, where water from a high tide is lying in pools, or on shelving sand between high and low tide.

Remember about INCOMING TIDE. Try to work out how high the tide will be by looking at the strand line where shells and flotsam from the high tide are washed up. Watch to see if the water is going in or out. High and low tide are six hours apart, and the maximum change in water height between tides in the Western Isles is about 4 metres. Look out for UNDERTOWS. If in doubt, don't bathe or even paddle, certainly not without an adult. (And don't throw sticks for dogs either, if you're not sure it's safe.)

The more exposed a beach is to waves and wind, the fewer creatures you will find living in the intertidal zone. However, there is plenty of food in the surfy water, and many other creatures, particularly filter feeders, live in the sand offshore which is permanently covered by water, to escape the constant disturbance of the tides. You won't see signs of the living animals on the beach, but you will find their shells washed up. In fact, you may spend hours collecting them!

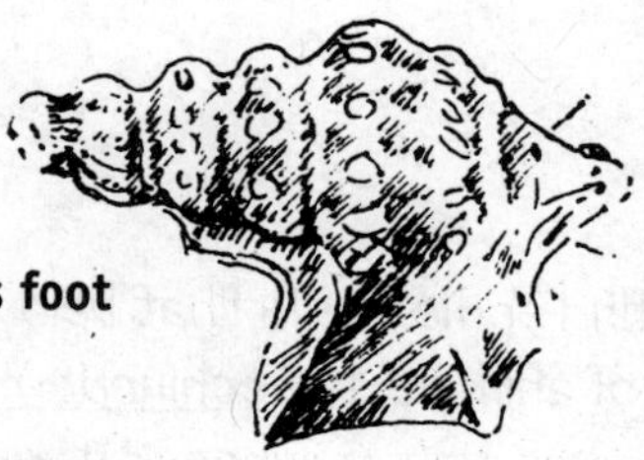

pelican's foot

blue-rayed limpet, brown with bright turquoise lines, lives in tangle holdfasts in deeper water

tower shell, this one has been borrowed!

cowrie

otter shell

Specially colourful are the salmon-pink **thin tellin**, the brilliant yellow or violet **banded wedge shell**, and the orange or crimson striped **tiger scallop**. These are all small bivalves of sandy shores. Pile your small shells inside the large ones – **otter shells, scallops** and **Iceland clams** make the best containers. Shells filled with shells look just as pretty as the exotic shells you see for sale in shops. It's not a good idea to buy these anyway – they are usually obtained by killing the live animal, and some species are now in danger as a result.

All the shells mentioned so far belonged to molluscs, soft-bodied creatures. The bivalves have two shells hinged together, though these separate after the animal dies. The molluscs that have only one shell are gastropods – which means they walk on their stomachs! If you think of the garden snail, which is related, you'll see the point.

Murder!

Look for shells with a small hole bored in them. This is a murder clue!

Some gastropods such as the necklace shell have a nasty habit of boring through shells with their file-like mouthparts and eating the inhabitants.

Bivalve shells which have no holes and are still joined at the hinge, but open, have probably been a wader's breakfast.

If you inspect the sand on a west coast beach, you'll find it's almost entirely made up of tiny fragments of shell. Draw a saucer-sized circle in the sand and look very closely at the colours of the individual grains. Can you tell which shells they came from? If you can't, cheat a bit – look at the whole shells on the strandline and match the colours.

Even from miles away, you can tell something about what lives off shore, from the overall colour of the beach. Cockles make very white sand, thin tellins make it pinky golden, like Scarista in Harris, lots of banded wedge shells make a pale yellow sand, mussels (living on nearby rocks) make blue-black streaks.

urchin alert

You'll find some shells that belong to a different order of animals, the echinodermata or spiny-skins – yes, you've guessed it, **sea urchins**.

Sea urchins can't actually see at all: they have no eyes. They can move about though, on five rows of tiny tube-feet which protrude from the outer shell or test. The five rows mark the sections you see on the empty shells of all types of sea urchin.

The urchin you're mostly likely to find on a sandy beach is one which (like so many residents of exposed beaches) lives buried in the sand just off shore – the **sea potato**. Not much good for making chips – but alive or recently dead it does look rather like a smallish brown potato. Once thoroughly dead, the test turns white. If you hunt carefully among the tiniest shells on the strandline, you might also find the minute white **pea urchin** – pea sized! But a rather squashed pea, as it's almost flat, not round. Look for these five fine lines to be sure it is an echinoderm.

what's in a name?

Usually a bit of history! **Razor shells** look just like an old-fashioned cut-throat razor, Sweeney Todd style. The **necklace shell** isn't a shell which is used to make necklaces. It gets its name from its spiral egg-mass, stuck together with sand, which dries to form a sand 'necklace' 2 – 3cm wide and about 10cm long. You may find some on the beach.

The **hermit crab** hides in its borrowed shell like a solitary holy man in his cave or cell.

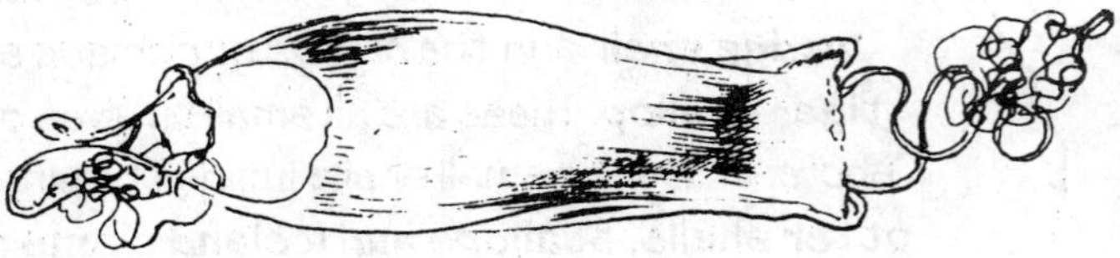

The egg cases of dogfish and rays are called **mermaid's purses** from the days when ladies kept their money in little drawstring bags. The urchin in **sea urchin** is an old word for hedgehog.

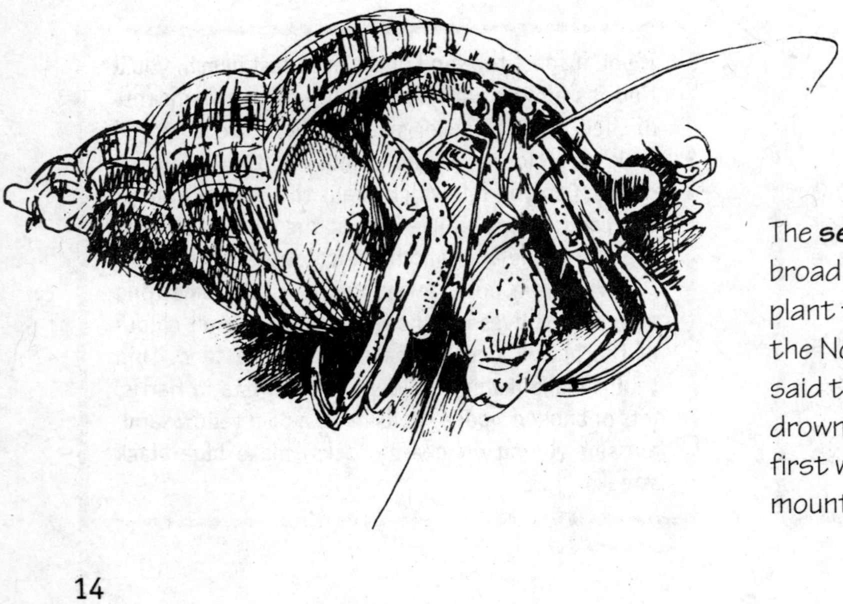

The **sea bean** looks like a huge shiny dark brown broad bean (about 5 x 8cm) It's the seed of a plant from the West Indies, which floats here with the North Atlantic Drift. In the Hebrides it was said that if you carried a seabean you would never drown, because the beans float so well. When boys first went to sea, they were sometimes given one mounted in silver.

Starfish are also echinoderms. Starfish aren't spiny, merely rough. The animal's fivefold structure, seen in the five 'arms' of most types of starfish as well as in urchins, is the clue to their relationship. In starfish, the tube-feet are arranged in lines under each 'arm'. If you get a chance to look at either urchins or starfish under water, you'll see the waving lines of semi-transparent tubes, which propel the animal along by water pressure.

In summer, look out too for **jellyfish** washed up on the shore. They aren't fish: in fact the more complex species aren't single animals at all, but colonies of simple organisms, in which individuals do different tasks – stinging, digesting, swimming and so on.The 'jelly' is mainly water, and after a few hours in the sun there will be nothing left but a faint coloured pattern on the sand. The most common jellyfish, with its four violet coloured segments, is completely harmless to humans. The big reddish brown **lion's mane**, though, has long tentacles which sting like nettles, so is best avoided. In August and September, you may also find the tiny bluish **by-the-wind sailor**, which has a triangular 'sail' poking above the surface of the water, and gets driven here by south-west winds from warmer waters.

Jellyfish are eaten by many other creatures and are the favourite food of **turtles**. Unfortunately, plastic bags and burst balloons look quite like jellyfish, and can injure or kill. So never dump polythene bags, even the smallest, in the sea or on the shore, and don't let balloons drift away, particularly those filled with helium which may travel for many miles. They look pretty, but could be death to wildlife.

REMEMBER – The sea is not our dustbin – it's home to countless living things.

Starfish can't live for long out of water, but sometimes you see dried-up dead ones on the shore. Your Mum might find the bigger ones a bit smelly, but if you're a patient shell-hunter, you may turn up a small **brittle star** – very pretty and guaranteed not to pong! These live almost anywhere, often in dense beds of millions of individuals, even where the seabed has been greatly disturbed.

Not all starfish have five arms! But they can all regrow any they lose, like this **sunstar**.

by-the-wind-sailor

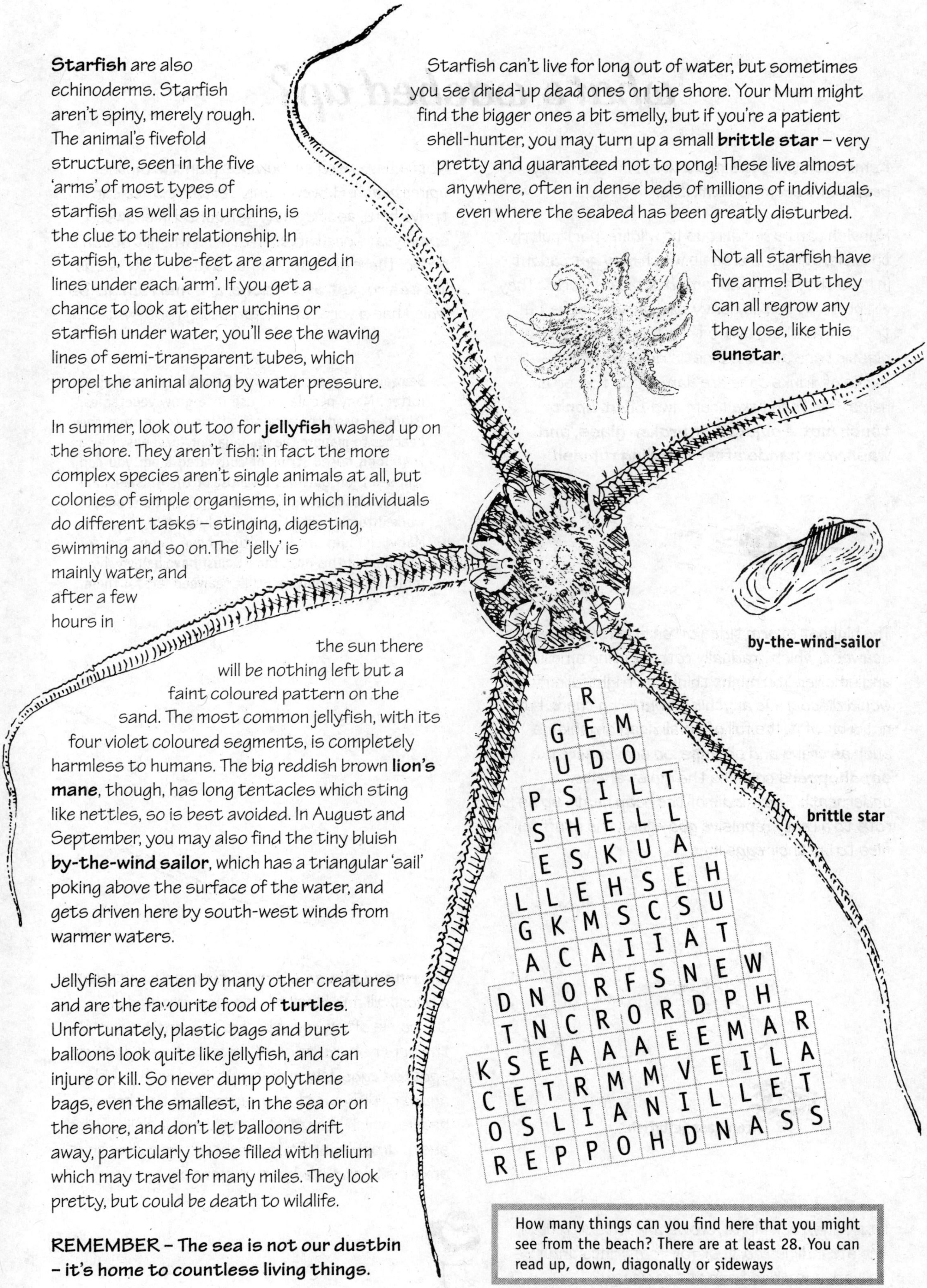

brittle star

R
G E M
U D O
P S I L T
S H E L L
E S K U A
L L E H S E H
G K M S C S U
A C A I I A T
D N O R F S N E W
T N C R O R D P H
K S E A A A E E M A R
C E T R M M V E I L A
O S L I A N I L L E T
R E P P O H D N A S S

How many things can you find here that you might see from the beach? There are at least 28. You can read up, down, diagonally or sideways

what's washed up?

Remember, the sea's not a dustbin? Too many people still seem to think it is.

Rubbish can be dangerous to wildlife, particularly to birds, otters and seals which may get caught in it as they swim. Discarded nets are worst. They will probably be too heavy for you to remove, but try to drag them above the strandline. Twine, plastic bags and the plastic rings from four-packs of drinks cans are dangerous too, so it helps if you can take them away. **But don't touch metal objects or broken glass, and wash your hands after handling rubbish.**

The highest storm tides often bring in masses of seaweed, which gradually rots, getting smellier and smellier. You might think the frightful niff would discourage anything from living there, but not a bit of it. It's full of small dead organisms such as crabs and shrimps, so scavengers like **sandhoppers** colonise the moist shelter underneath. The middle of the heap heats up as it rots to a really repulsive goo – just the stuff for flies to lay their eggs in.

compass jellyfish

Starlings, rock pipits, crows and rats all dine on the strandline too. Look for footprints and try to work out who's been at the party.

Rotted seaweed encourages plantlife on the upper beach. However, only certain plants can thrive here, as they may get buried in seaweed some years or starved in others when it doesn't arrive. There are a few annuals with hardy seeds like **sea rocket** and **orache**, and **marram grass** which has a very tough, spreading root system.

Seaweed is an excellent fertiliser, particularly when rotted. Many people still use it to grow vegetables. Islanders used to carry off all they could from the beaches to manure the feanagan or 'lazybeds'. These were long raised strips of cultivated land: you can still see their outlines on most of the hillsides and on tiny offshore islands, showing how hard people worked to cultivate such unlikely places.
Many changes in agriculture have been bad for wildlife, but this one at least must have helped shore birds, who now have all that seaweed left for them.

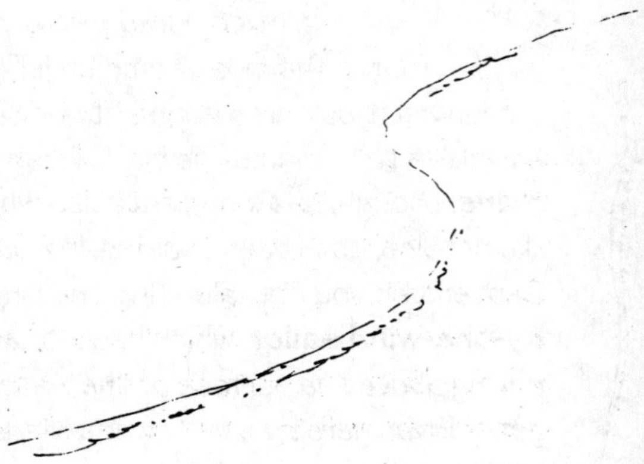

The **ringed plover** is dumpy, fawn and white, with a short bill and black bib. Its clear piping call 'tooee', is often heard before the bird is seen. On the upper shore, be careful not to tread on their spotted eggs, laid in a scrape lined with pebbles and very difficult to see, or on their tiny brown babies, which 'freeze' at danger and look like dried sheep droppings! If the parents keep calling that anxious 'tooee!' it's best to move on.

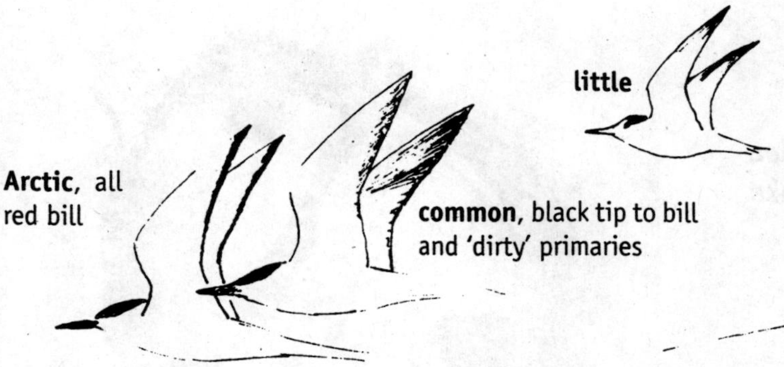

Arctic terns are much more common here than **common terns**. Very alike ! **Little terns** are smaller, paler with a black-tipped yellow bill. All three species fish in skimming dives, catching mostly sandeels.

Terns are summer visitors, dainty white birds with forked tails. Terns nest colonially, often on bare sand or pebbles on the upper shore. If you find yourself in a tern colony, leave quickly (they may help you on your way by divebombing!) and watch quietly from a distance – terns get very distressed by intruders, and may desert their eggs, or have them stolen by gulls while they are intent on seeing off humans.

Dunlin are winter visitors on most of Britain's coasts, but also breed in the Western Isles. Two-tone buffy grey in winter, rich brown upperparts barred with black and a jet-black waistcoat in summer.

Oystercatcher black and white with red beak and orange legs. One oystercatcher can eat about 300 cockles in a day! The Gaelic name gille bridean means 'St Brigid's servant'.

Waders love the bugs in rotted seaweed especially **turnstones**, attractive tortoiseshell-patterned little birds which turn seaweed as well as stones.

beach garlands

Children at Lochmaddy School adapted the idea of artist Chris Drury and used flotsam to make garlands telling a story of a walk round their local loch. Theirs was a brackish loch, so they used plaited rushes as a base to weave their finds into, but you could do the same thing on a beachcombing walk, perhaps using cast-up twine or netting as a base. Then add objects, both natural and man-made, that will remind you of the beach – feathers, dried seaweed, small polystyrene floats, shells, whatever takes your fancy.

At the very top of most beaches there are sand dunes. They are the border between land and sea. The roots of marram are what hold them there – otherwise the sand would blow away before other plants got a chance to establish themselves. The marram's roots act like netting. But dunes are an unstable system: chunks get washed away in winter storms, then the front of the dune has no marram to protect it, and wind will blow the sand inland, sometimes feet deep. On the island of Boreray there is an old village buried in the sand. Dunes formed over the houses, and later collapsed again during further storms, revealing the ruins. On the RSPB bird reserve at Balranald in North Uist, where a track runs behind the dunes, you can see distinct layers of sand and humus, where the dunes stabilised for a while, grew a cover of plants, and were buried in more blown sand – several times!

Dune erosion can be a serious nuisance to crofters, so try not to be part of the problem. Anything that breaks up the marram root-mat hastens erosion – and that could include you!

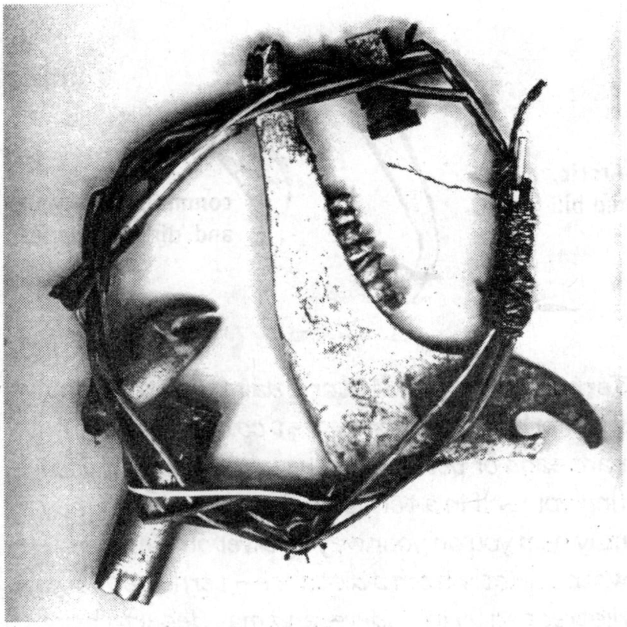

There's plenty to do on the beach, but there are some things you shouldn't do:

DON'T:
jump heavily down dunes (otters do, but you know better, right?)
drive on the dunes or beach
leave litter
break glass
take home live specimens (or those you have robbed of life for the purpose...)
go in the sea without an adult
inspect unexploded bombs

Can you think of more 'don'ts'? Why not try your hand at a Sand Shockers Limerick?

Some kids, with a yell and a screech
Found a strange-looking Thing on the beach
They poked it and flicked it
And threw it...
...and kicked it
And vapourised all within reach!

3. The machair

Too much blowing sand from eroding dunes can bury pasture: but if no sand blew inland, the unique habitat called machair in Gaelic wouldn't be there at all. It's the grassy plain behind the dunes, rich in flowering plants. Machair occurs only in north-west Scotland and Ireland, where you find the magic ingredient – shell sand, pounded by Atlantic breakers and blown by Atlantic gales.

Shell sand is calcareous – lime rich. It sweetens the acid, peaty soil of the islands and at the same time drains it, so that it warms up more quickly in Spring. As a result, though bleak and scoured by sand and salty winds in winter, the machair is transformed in summer into a spectacular flowery meadow. The loveliest machair is where grazing and cultivation are most carefully managed, as at Eoligarry, Vatersay and Balranald.

Some of the drawings in this section are from field notes kept by children from Leverburgh. They visited the machair at Northton because that was where the naturalist William MacGillivray lived when he was young. MacGillivray recorded many of the same birds in his own journal in 1817.

Lochs often form behind the dunes, which act as a barrier, or at the landward edge of the machair plain where water drains from the peaty hillsides. These machair lochs are quite special. They are usually shallow, and brackish (slightly salty) from spray and salt winds.

Because of the shell-sand, they aren't acid like moorland lochs. Look for the dainty white flowers and feathery leaves of **water crowfoot**, and the showy yellow splashes of **kingcup.** The machair water is rich in nutrients and supports great numbers of invertebrates, especially **water beetles** and the larvae of **mayflies** and **caddisflies**.

Swans are the most spectacular residents of these lochs. The waterweeds which particularly like the brackish, shallow conditions are ideal food for them. **Mute swans** breed in the Uists in large numbers and **whooper swans** visit for the winter.

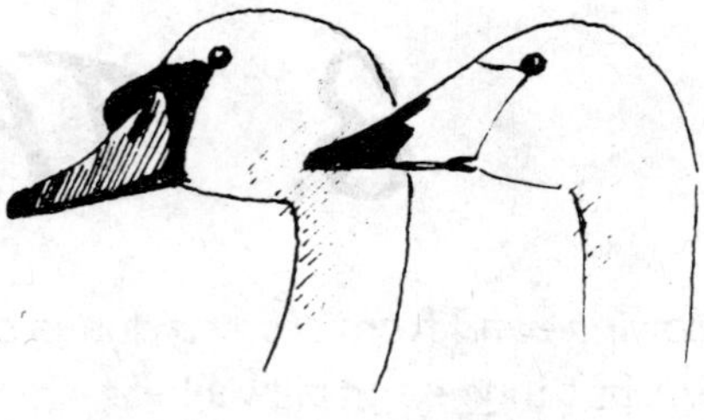

mute swan very large, gracefully curved neck, orange red bill with a black knob at the base, larger in the male, upturned tail.

whooper swan smaller, with straighter neck and yellow and black bill – no knob. Flight-call a musical bugling rather than a whoop.

Mute swans don't nest north of the Sound of Harris, probably because the ideal brackish conditions for bringing up cygnets are far less common there than in the Uists. So if you want to see cygnets, go to the Uists.

milkwort

bird's foot trefoil

The machair is definitely the place for flower freaks! Early July is the most colourful time. In dry places you'll find **bird's foot trefoil, lady's bedstraw, thyme, white clover** and **yarrow.** In cultivated places and bare ground look for **common storksbill, forget me not, longheaded poppy,** and **silverweed.** Damp areas have **ragged robin, spotted** and **marsh orchids, yellow flag iris** and **meadowsweet.** There are dozens of others – have fun with the ticklist at the back of the book.

Hebridean orchid

northern marsh orchid

In a crofting township each house sits on its own croft. But as well as this, the township has common land. Townships with machair in their common land still sometimes grow crops there. In the past, when people had to grow enough to feed themselves and their animals through the winter, this was always done. The best parts of the machair were divided into long strips, and every family was given a share.

Not all the strips were used every year. Because the machair soil is light and dry, it has to be given a rest between crops, so crofters practised a rotation of potatoes in the first year, oats the next year, and two or three years fallow (no crop). Grazing animals were kept off the machair for most of the summer.

Where this system is still used, as at Balranald, you can see very clearly what a variety of flowers it makes. In the first year of fallow, the sandy soil is almost bare, and annuals such as **dead nettle**, **longheaded poppy** and **corn marigold** can seed and grow successfully. By the second year there is more grass, so less room for annuals, but still plenty of space for small shallow-rooted plants like **wild pansy**. By the third year the bare soil is mostly covered by vegetation, and deeper-rooted plants like **wild carrot**, **self-heal** and **yarrow** are getting established again.

The crops and fallows of different years stripe the machair with bands of contrasting brilliant colour. Not only does it look and smell beautiful, biodiversity is greater, because the huge variety of plants increases the range of insects and birds which can feed and breed there.

The machair is a very special wildlife habitat – but it is not 'wild'. For centuries, people grazed sheep and cattle on the flower-rich pasture, and cultivated strips for oats and potatoes. Without any grazing, the strongest plants like ragwort and knapweed take over, and dead grass (especially **red fescue**) forms mats in winter, smothering more delicate plants. However, too much grazing is not good for the machair either: the more delicate things get pulled up by the roots, and coarse plants which sheep don't like, such as **ragwort** and **burdock**, increase and crowd out the rest. These coarse plants have thick taproots which reach far down into the soil, rather than a network of shallow roots spreading outwards, so wind can more easily loosen the top surface and cause erosion. Cattle help the machair because they don't pull out roots, and because their droppings are good manure and spread seeds.

common storksbill

silverweed

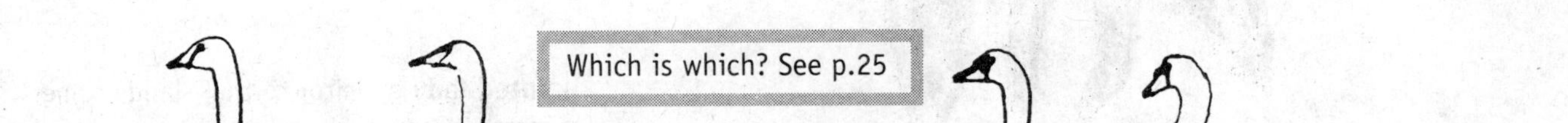

Which is which? See p.25

bugs and butterflies

You probably think of 'a beetle' or 'a spider' or 'an earthworm' or 'a snail'. But sixteen different types of worm have been recorded on the machair, numerous spiders and small snails, and hundreds of different types of beetle! Add to this flies, ants, aphids, bees, moths and butterflies, and the larvae of all these, and you can tell this is a paradise for insect-eating birds. But – good news – midges are discouraged by the sea breezes and dry soil of the machair – though not completely, mind you!

Clue: butterflies can fold their wings together up over their backs. Moths wings usually fold against their bodies.

angle shades moth
around late in the year – September

Hebrew character moth looks as if it has writing on its wings; emerges April

puss moth
May: large horned caterpillars feed on willow

large white
greenish white with dark spots on forewing. Food plants, cabbage family, wild and cultivated.

Other butterflies you might see include:
small tortoiseshell bright orange and black, blue spotted border to wings. Food plant nettles.
common blue male bright violety-blue, female brownish with orange spots. Underside silvery with orange spots. Food plant clover.
meadow brown grey brown with orange on forewings. Food plant grasses.
large heath the one on the front cover: orangey brown with black 'eye' on forewing.

Children from Carinish made a printed banner, using polystyrene blocks they had cut with outlines of birds, flowers and bugs. If you want to try this you need to use fairly thick paint, so the cut lines don't fill up with it, otherwise they won't show up when you print.

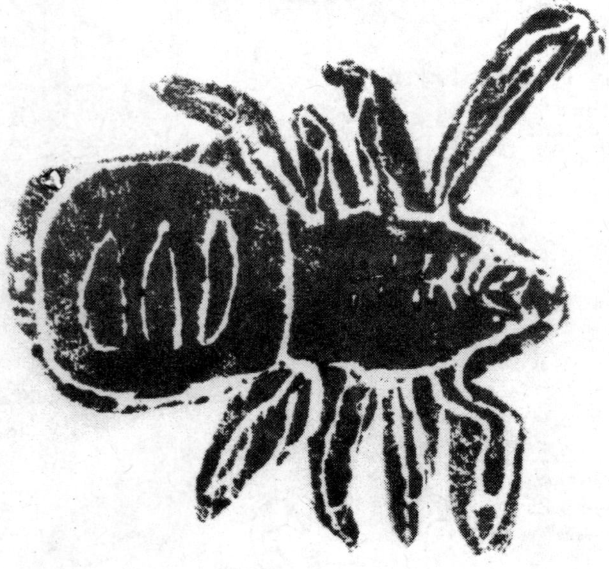

painted lady a visitor to the islands some summers. Gorgeously coloured – orange with black and white. Fast flying.

s.b.j.'s and others

twite smallest and plumpest, very short bill, bounces through the air saying 'twit!' in a self-satisfied tone

meadow pipit this is the one that isn't anything else!

skylark slimmer, slight crest, glorious song

corn bunting, much plumper, chunky bill, perches on fences near cultivation jingling like a bunch of keys

Have you heard of **S.B.J.'s** – small brown jobs, the birdwatcher's headache? The machair is full of them!

Most birds, even seed-eaters, need the concentrated protein of animal food when they are breeding, to build up the strength of the female before she lays her eggs and to feed the chicks. So the <u>invertebrates</u> of the machair attract huge numbers of nesting birds.

Oystercatchers and **ringed plover** nest in the dry machair as well as on the upper shore. The damp areas with some puddles and tussocks are ideal for other waders such as **dunlin**, **lapwing** and **snipe**. **Redshanks** favour a bit of cover from flag iris.

snipe

Shelduck like old rabbit burrows, of which there are usually plenty on the machair. But there really isn't much choice of where to nest for machair birds!

There are no natural ground predators to bother them, so nesting on the ground shouldn't be a problem. But in the last thirty years, a number of newcomers have become a menace. **Mink** escaped from fur farms, and are now having to be trapped to save crofters' poultry and ground-nesting birds in Lewis and Harris. **Hedgehogs** were brought in because they eat garden pests and look 'sweet': so they are, but they do love eggs and chicks! **Polecat ferrets** were let loose on the bird reserve at Balranald to control **rabbits** – themselves a human introduction.

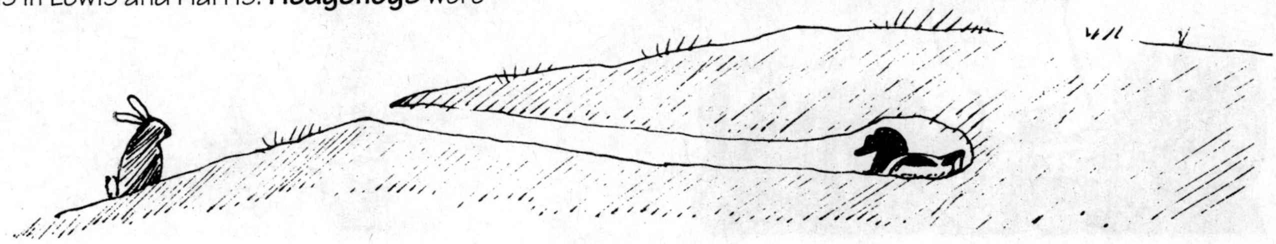

history of a cowpat

Splat! A nice warm steaming heap in the grass! There's still lots of nourishment here, vegetable matter partly broken down by the cow's digestive system. Within minutes, it's being sized up by **dungflies**, which resemble reddish-brown bluebottles. Tasty! And just the place to lay eggs, providing the next generation with a food-store.

The **earthworm** most important to the machair, lumbricus rubellus, is a much smaller species than the ones in your garden. A real pioneer – forging out even into the dunes, encouraged by fresh juicy cowpats! They're a favourite snack for **lapwings** to bring to their chicks.

The great naturalist Charles Darwin thought worms were the best thing out! They are vital to the health of soil. Their burrowing habits draw organic matter (basically, dead stuff that was once living – leaves, dung or corpses!) down into the inorganic layer (sand in this case) so that plants have something to feed on.

Along comes a **dung beetle**, or maybe two. Several species of dung beetle lead model family lives: Mum and Dad roll a ball of dung into a burrow to provide food for their expected offspring, then she lays her eggs beside it, and they both guard the nest till the larvae hatch. The ancient Egyptians were so impressed by the hard work of the dung beetle or 'scarab', rolling its ball of dung to give life to its children, that they made it the symbol of the sungod, rolling the sun across the sky to give life to all creatures.

Lie in the grass with your eyes shut for the biodiversity test! How many different natural sounds can you hear? How many scents can you pick out? Feel the ground. Can you tell which plants you are touching?

You can turn this into a game.

Everyone in turn is blindfolded, rolled over several times, has a hand placed on a plant by the others (NOT a thistle!) and has to say what it is. If the first guess isn't correct, the guesser can ask up to ten questions to help - only 'yes-or-no' answers allowed. For example,'Is it in flower?' 'Has it got more than five petals?' 'Does it smell nice?'

The pat is drying out now in the sun and wind. Here's a flock of **starlings** 'Ooh! Cor, look at them maggots, we go a bundle on them!' The starlings' table manners ensure bits of cowpat have been scattered about, fertilising the nearby plants, and letting air in to dry and break up the pat further. Here comes a **pied wagtail** to pick up the tiny insects scattered with the remains of the feast.

Now it's just right as a home for **red ants**. They're great food for the young of nesting **meadow pipits** and **skylarks.** Youch!! Look out for that **merlin**!

Not much left of that cowpat by now. After the rain and frost of winter it will have disappeared entirely. But next Spring the grass and leaves where it lay will be a brighter, healthier green, and one or two different species may be added to this little patch of dry machair – maybe a damp-loving plant like cuckoo flower, grown from seed which passed undigested through the cow and got a rich, moist start in life.

Can you make a food-web diagram out of the cowpat story?

Machair <u>ecology</u> is a complicated network. Sometimes it's not obvious at first what is happening.

Rabbits were introduced to the islands for food. They became a nuisance on the machair, as their burrows undermine the fragile vegetation and can cause serious erosion. They also compete for grazing with sheep. Myxomatosis, a horrible disease, was introduced to curb the rabbits. Since then no-one has fancied eating the rabbits at all – so the few that survive the disease breed till there are huge numbers again. A new myxomatosis epidemic happens every few years, so there is <u>boom and bust</u> in the rabbit population. The disease seems to be worst after a frosty winter. Why? Probably it's because it's spread by **fleas.** In long frosty spells rabbits spend more time huddled in their burrows, where the fleas breed, and less grooming themselves. **Buzzards** feed mostly on rabbits, so while there are plenty of rabbits, you will see lots of buzzards, but in the year after an epidemic there will be far fewer. All a bit like the old lady who swallowed a fly, then a spider to catch the fly, and so on...

In any <u>ecosystem</u> the various species have adapted over time to 'fit in', each finding its own <u>niche</u> in terms of food and territory. A new species moving in suddenly can cause disaster.

Incomers are brought by humans, either deliberately or accidentally – but usually thoughtlessly. Of course, not all introductions succeed. Take frogs: lots of people have brought spawn and tadpoles from the mainland, hoping the frogs would DO SOMETHING about midges. But the frogs never survive, no-one knows why.

Maybe it's just as well – we might end up with Killer Frogs mopping up the thingies that keep midge larvae down. Remember what happened to the old lady at the end of the song? She's dead, of course!

One introduction that doesn't seem to have done any harm is the **Prince's Flower** – said to have grown from seed brought by Bonny Prince Charlie, when he was a fugitive after the 1745 rebellion. You can find it on Eriskay and Vatersay. Can you spot it on the front cover?

4. Round the croft

Crofting villages are often built where the sandy machair runs up against the rocky spine of the island with its skin of peaty moorland. The soil here is darker and damper than the machair, and though the crofts in summer are bright with many of the same wildflowers, the habitat is somewhat different. For a start, it is a human habitat too, so anything else using the area mustn't be too fazed by human clatter, or by dogs, cats, and livestock. There are niches for bold opportunists like starlings, and for others which benefit from a particular food or type of shelter to be found near our dwellings, like corncrakes. It all adds to biodiversity!

Around the beginning of last century, the old settlements were cleared of people to make way for big sheep farms. The crofting system as we know it was set up to right the injustice of these 'Clearances'. The large farms were split up into 'townships' to give each family enough ground to support themselves with two cows, some sheep, and ground for crops. These new townships were spread out, with each house set in its own land. In some villages you can still see the low drystone ruins of the older houses, clustered close together and almost overgrown, often much nearer the sea than the present houses. Sollas in North Uist is a good example. The old village is a huddle of ruins right down on the machair, while the newer crofthouses run in a straggling line where the ground begins to rise to the hillside behind – the 'blackland'.

The children of lochdar School investigated foodwebs as part of their entry for the wildlife competition. They found their local top predator was the domestic cat.

This is bad news for **corncrakes**, which not only nest on the ground, but spend most of their time there. Because the habitat corncrakes need is nearly always found near villages, they can't get away from cats.

Cats kill enormous numbers of small birds in Britain every year. If you have cats, you can help by having your pets neutered so that unwanted kittens don't feralise – that is, go wild. If cats are left to fend for themselves they naturally kill more than a well-fed moggy needs to bother with.

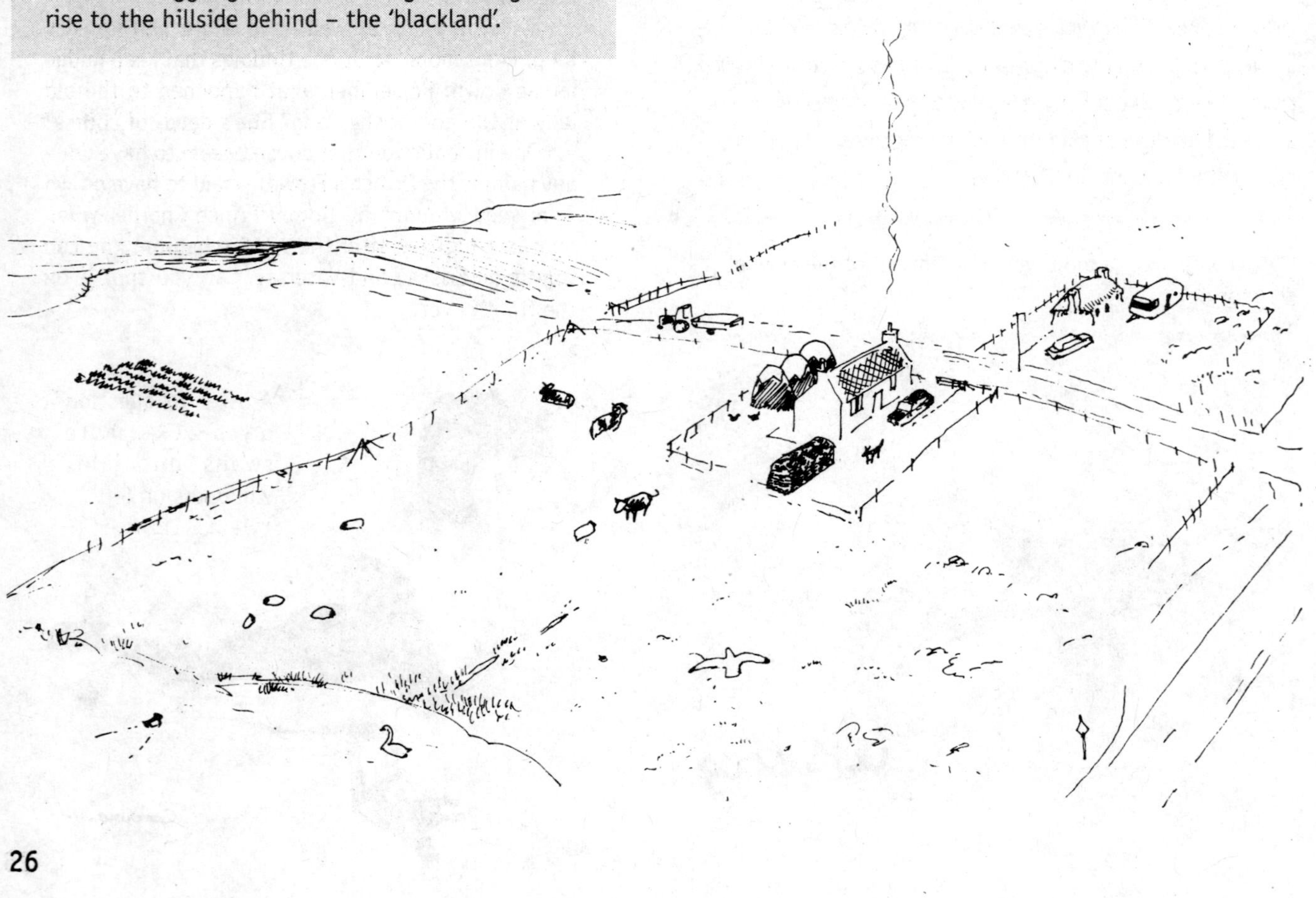

a voice in the night

The **corncrake** is star of the show in the machair townships . Corncrakes are very secretive and unless tragedy occurs they are seldom seen...

...but they are frequently heard!

Some of the best places to hear corncrakes are Eoligarry in Barra and the Balranald bird reserve in North Uist. Listen – use your binoculars, you may be lucky – but don't tramp around looking for the noisemaker. It is against the law to harrass this rare bird, but apart from that, it's very unkind, because they are easily scared away and there may be nowhere else for them to nest.

The male crakes most of the day and all of the night throughout the breeding season, and any rival within earshot crakes back. Everyone loves the corncrake because it's the bird of summer, but you feel like throwing a boot at it by the time it's kept you awake till 3 a.m.

Corncrakes spend the winters in Africa, arriving in Europe to breed from late April onwards. Male corncrakes choose an area of suitable habitat big enough to provide enough insect food to feed a family. Once he has found a good spot, the male crakes, which lets females know he's there and looking for a mate, and other males know his patch is occupied.

Corncrakes like to skulk in rank meadow vegetation. Damp ground on the edge of the machair with flag irises, knapweed and meadow sweet, and a ditch if possible, is just the place for a corncrake, and that's what an old-fashioned hay meadow is like. They are now terribly endangered, because modern agriculture has almost banished this habitat from Europe. The Hebrides and Ireland are last strongholds. Conservationists are doing everything they can to help the corncrake. Traditional crofting is a vital part of the scheme. Putting livestock off the fields to let vegetation grow in the spring, then mowing it very late in the summer for hay instead of cutting for silage in June, and working from the centre of a field to its edges to allow the young birds to escape, are ways to help. So if you notice overgrown, untidy fields around the crofts, it doesn't mean no-one's bothering – they may be Corncrake Corners, actual or potential.

geese and grass

Many crofts are heavily grazed for most of the year. They may be reseeded from time to time, or have fertiliser applied. This produces just the sort of short grass that **greylag geese** like. But crofters don't always like geese on their pasture. Various goose scaring devices help to keep them off – till they get used to them!

Greylags breed at Loch Druidibeg in South Uist, a reserve which was set up for their benefit, and on the small islands in the Sound of Harris. The parent birds pair for life. The young ones stay with them in a family group through the winter, and sometimes much longer. You can pick out the different families when they are flying or grazing, because each clusters near Dad, who is biggest, and often stands tall keeping a watchful eye open for danger, while the others have their heads down grazing.

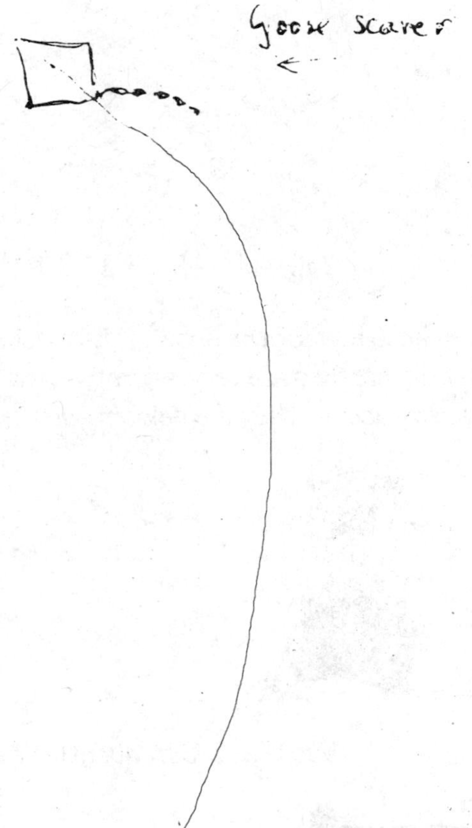

The greylag is by far the likeliest goose you'll see, the only one in summer. Some **pinkfooted geese** and **Greenland whitefronted geese** pass through the islands in winter. They are migrants, which nest far beyond the Arctic circle. They are 'grey geese' too, like the greylags. (Actually they're all greyish brown: greylags are the largest, with lighter heads and necks.)

Barnacle geese visit pasture land in winter too: they are 'black' geese, though in fact it's only the neck which is black, with white face and grey body, lighter underneath. You might think they got their name from eating barnacles, but geese are vegetarians. The name comes from a tall old story that ship's barnacles were the young of this coastal goose. Well, the barnacles do look slightly like a cracking eggshell, with a stalk that *might* remind you of a goose's neck.

SEASONS

The answer to each of the questions is the name of a month. All the answers can be worked out from information somewhere in this book. CLUE: The initial letters of the right months will give you the name of a seashore creature which isn't mentioned elsewhere. Answers in mirror writing at side of page.

1. See by-the-wind sailors in —
2. Hebrew character moth emerges in—
3. Grey seal pups are weaned in—
4. Barnacle geese drop by in—
5. Gull chicks hatch in—
6. Crowberry feeds moorland birds in—
7. Angle shades moth is around in—
8. Redwings pass through in—
9. A lot of rain falls in—

ANSWERS: September, April, November, December, May, August, September, October, November – SANDMASON.

an eagle on a gatepost?

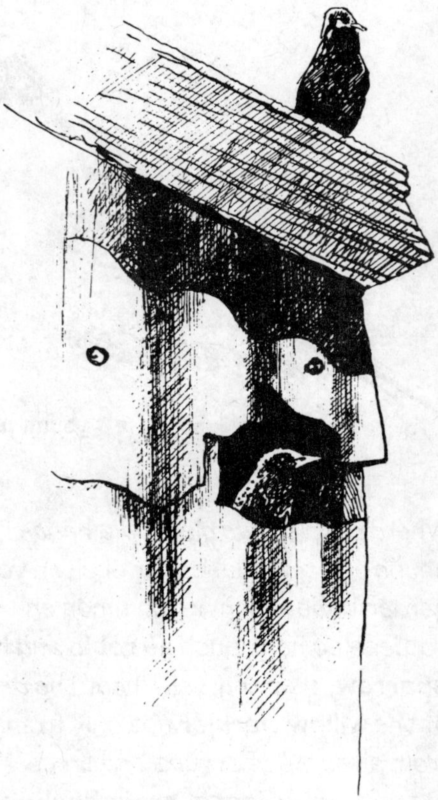

Another very different bird which enjoys the croftland is the **starling**. They're common, but don't take them for granted: the starlings of Shetlkand and the Hebrides are a different subspecies from the mainland starling, slightly spottier and glossier. More importantly, they do a great job letting air into the soil, which helps break down dead organic material into useful humus. The bare, cropped winter pasture has a rich layer of worms, insects and pupae just under the surface. Flocks of starlings whiz in, chattering and exclaiming, and waddle up and down probing for food. They open their conical bills inside the holes, and then squint down to see if they're in luck. If not – they're off again, all in a tight black flock.

Come summer, the starlings are still there. You see them sitting on the backs of the sheep, teasing out wool, and zooming off to line their nests with the stolen strand. They nest in crevices, including some unlikely places – old tractor tyres, empty oildrums, derelict cars and postboxes, to name a few! You can detect a starling nest from the loud wheezing chirps of the babies demanding food. They're not very musical – and neither are their parents. However, starlings are very good mimics, and if you don't realise you're near a male starling in his nesting territory, you'll get some surprises. Can there really be a cat or a motorbike or a shepherd whistling his dog up on the chimney pot, or a golden eagle on the gatepost? Maybe the variety of new noises is one reason starlings like hanging round houses!

People are often surprised to find starlings in the islands, because they think of them as town birds. Not a bit of it! Until about two hundred years ago, starlings were not that common in mainland Britain. Then came the growth of the towns, and starlings soon realised there were good pickings to be had, and that the new urban and industrial landscapes offered plenty of crevices for nesting in. They became quite a serious pest in places. In the British countryside, they are now declining because of modern agricultural methods, but in the islands traditional crofting keeps them in business. It's as important for the common starling as for the rare corncrake.

how does the garden grow?

young **pied wagtail**

Where people have planted a hedge round the house or a few bushes for shelter, you'll find the garden birds which are common on the mainland, but less so here, such as **robin** and **house sparrow**. In spring, you'll hear the descending trill of the **willow warbler** not only from willows, but from all sorts of shrubs and trees. Fir-trees may attract **goldcrests, greenfinches** or **siskins**. Gardens provide food and shelter for the young of resident birds. They are also stopovers for migrating birds which don't breed here but need to stop for a rest on their long passages north in spring or south in autumn, like the **blackcap**. The commonest passage migrant is the **redwing**, a berry-eating bird of the thrush family, with orangey red 'armpits'. Look out for it in October and April.

blackcap in **sunbush**, a New Zealand shrub with yellow daisy flowers.

There's history to be read in the native plants around the crofts. Take **nettles** – you'd probably rather not, but in the days when food could only be preserved by salting, young nettles made a welcome fresh green broth, mixed with oatmeal, in spring. They thrive on decayed organic rubbish, so they're always to be found round henhouses, byres and rubbish heaps – wherever there has been human settlement. They are one of the earliest plants to come up green in spring. Several species of butterflies and moths depend on nettles as a food plant for their caterpillars.

You'll often find **tansy** and **mint** growing near old houses or on a village roadside. These herbs were used in tea, both to flavour it and for health reasons – they're good for the digestion.

Many plants were used in dyeing wool for home weaving. Until about thirty years ago, these were the dyes used in Harris tweed. For example, **flag iris** root gives a bluey green shade. **Crotal** is a lumpy grey lichen, black on the underside, which grows on the rocks on the hillside. It gives a rich reddish brown. It was said that you shouldn't wear anything dyed with crotal if you went to sea, because it would draw you back to the rocks.

Many of the plants which do best in Hebridean gardens aren't native varieties, but from abroad, even from much warmer climates: for example, **fuschia** (Africa), **pampas grass** (Argentina) **olearia** and **sunbush** (New Zealand) and **rugosa rose** (Japan). These grow because the islands don't get much frost. What they do suffer from is blasting salty winds, so foreign shrubs with very narrow or very tough leaves do better on the west side of the islands (the windiest) than even very hardy native trees like rowan and alder.

Planting 'exotics' is rather frowned on by conservationists these days, but in the special climate conditions of the islands it's a case of anything goes if you want a garden at all! Without the help of these unexpected exotics, there would hardly be any garden birds in the villages.

Perhaps the most powerful plant of all was the **bogbean**, which is found in the shallow lochans on the moors and between blackland and machair. It could cure just about everything and made a general tonic to stop you catching anything to start with! This plant too may prove to have real medical uses: modern medical researchers are beginning to realise that some old wives' tales were told by very wise old wives. **The children of Lochmaddy school did lots of research on the bogbean for the wildlife competition, and even got a recipe for the tonic.**

bogbean

St John's wort

Another plant with magical properties was **St John's wort**. It had to be happened upon, not looked for, but if you found it, it would protect you against all sorts of harm, and had healing powers. The plant does really have medical uses and makes a good soothing ointment.

Until about fifty years ago, people had to produce most of what they and their animals ate from the land. Their main crops were oats and potatoes. You may wonder how they could grow enough, in the short, cool, windy summers of the Western Isles. Of course, far more of the land was cultivated, as you can tell from the outlines of the old feanagan or lazybeds. But also, they grew different crop varieties which were late ripening, to take advantage of every bit of sunshine, and short-stemmed, to cope with wind, and which did well with organic manure and no artificial fertiliser. Occasionally crofters still grow a patch of the old 'blue' potatoes, which have dark purply skins. Ask around and see if anyone you know has come across these.

It's not only in the Hebrides that old varieties were suited to local conditions. The loss of such varieties is a worldwide trend – some plant scientists think a worldwide problem. Regulations make it difficult or even illegal for farmers to save their own seed, so wherever they live, they have to plant types evolved to suit modern high tech agricultural methods. The result is a great loss in biodiversity. This does not seem harmful as long as the new standard varieties don't succumb to new pests or diseases, but could be very serious if that happened; whereas with many different plant strains, some at least would probably be more resistant to any new disease.

Biodiversity doesn't just mean more wildlife to look at – it's a vital insurance for the future of the planet.

5. Peatbog and moorland

Sounds boring, doesn't it? Brown, squelchy and midge-infested.

But it isn't! Some of the weirdest wildlife is to be found here.

Carnivorous plants...

Peat is low in nutrients: these plants make up for it by digesting small insects they trap in their sticky leaves.

sundew

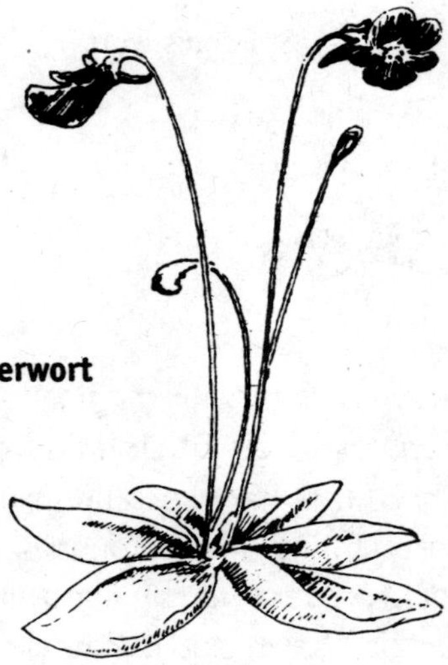

butterwort

'pirate' birds...

arctic skua chasing terns

Skuas are quite capable of catching their own fish but they prefer to chase other fishing birds, especially terns, and make them drop their catch. They nest on moors near the sea in Lewis. Look out! They divebomb intruders.

bonxie or **great skua**

viking voles…

The **field-vole** found in the Uists may be a Scandinavian subspecies. Its ancestors may have come in the Norsemen's longships. Rodents often travel this way, that's how they reached so many islands. Hope they don't get seasick!

dragons and damsels…

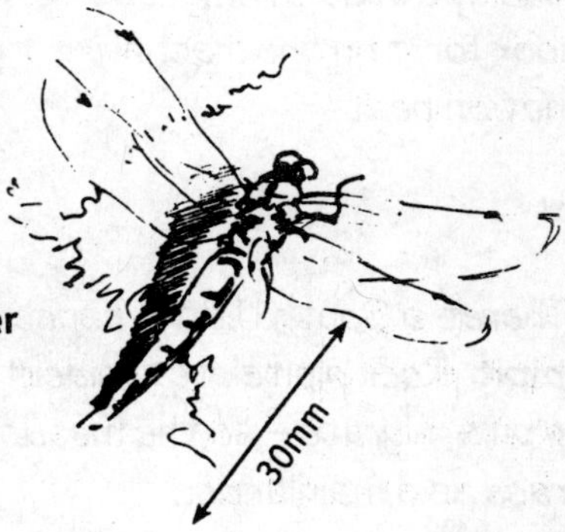

highland darter

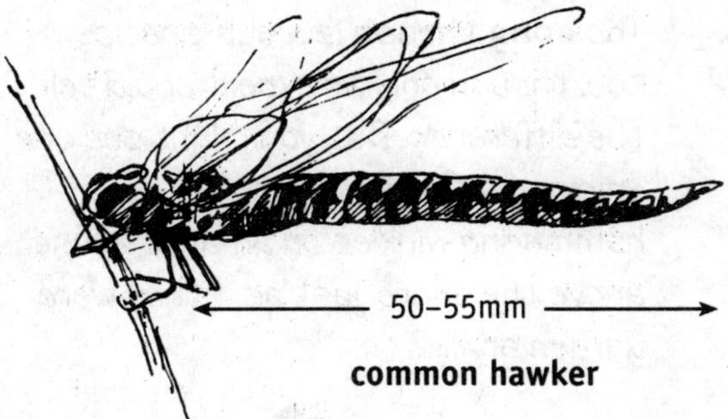

common hawker

Dragonflies are solitary hunters of smaller insects, very big, patrolling a stretch of water and ready to see off rivals. Dragonflies you might see here are **common hawkers** (large, with bright turquoise rings). The **highland darter**, **black darter** and **four-spotted chaser** are smaller, but fly in the same purposeful way – listen for their wings clashing!

blue-tailed damsel

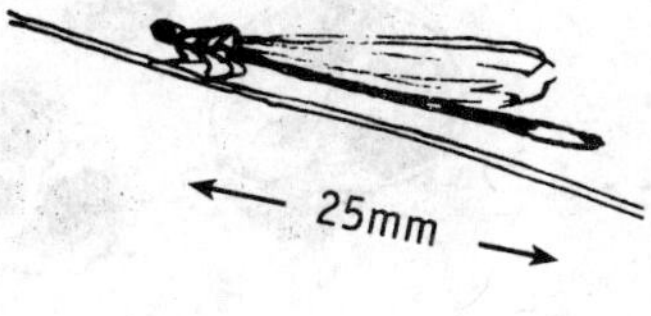

Damselflies are much more slender. You'll probably only notice them when they catch the light with a sudden glint of colour. You sometimes see swarms of them on warm July days. Look for **large red**, **blue-tailed** and **common blue** – all similar size, but coloured as their names indicate.

I ♥ peat bogs!

Nothing to see but buzzy insects and small brown birds? Find yourself a convenient seat on rock or a hummock of old dry heather and look again. What exactly is buzzing? A bumble bee? But what sort? Most likely one you won't see anywhere else – the furry orange **Hebridean bumble bee**.

It's only recently that people have come to realise that peatbogs are not only good for cutting fuel, not just fascinating places to watch wildlife, but immensely valuable in maintaining the earth. Like the tropical forests, they are carbon sinks: the plants mop up carbon dioxide which is produced from our burning of fossil fuels like coal and oil, helping to reduce global warming and consequent climate change.

Islands are great places for sub-species because creatures may be separated from their mainland relatives for thousands of years. Another Hebridean is the lovely crimson variety of the **spotted orchid**, but look for it on the machair, not on peat.

POND DIPPING

YOU NEED:

*a long handled dipping net
*an old margarine tub or similar
*a magnifying glass if you have one

1. Find a **SAFE** place to stand.
2. Put a little water in your tub.
3. Sweep your net through the water just below the surface in a figure of eight movement, without gathering mud from the bottom.
4. Transfer contents of net to tub.
5. Examine your catch.
6. Gently replace the creatures in the water, and repeat dipping from another spot.

If you can't identify anything, make notes and drawings. Does it swim, skate or crawl? How many legs? How many body segments? Size? Colour?

National Bog Day happens in July – look out for posters, there might be a bog event in your area!

There's a South Uist subspecies of the **rock pipit**. Rock pipits are resident, whereas meadow pipits migrate – so the meadow pipit is the same race as a mainlander.

The **song thrush** is a sub-species too, though only an expert could tell the difference. But you might see one enjoying a shellfish dinner – hammering winkles on an 'anvil' stone above the shore, just as if they were garden snails.

And you can't miss the **Hebridean wren** – slightly larger than a mainlander, but still a very small bird with a very loud voice!

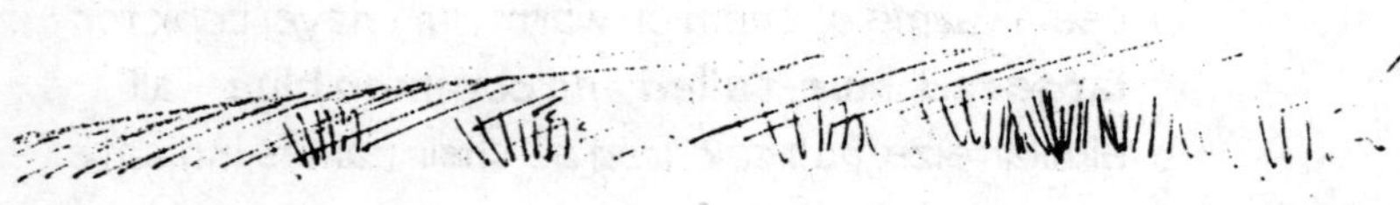

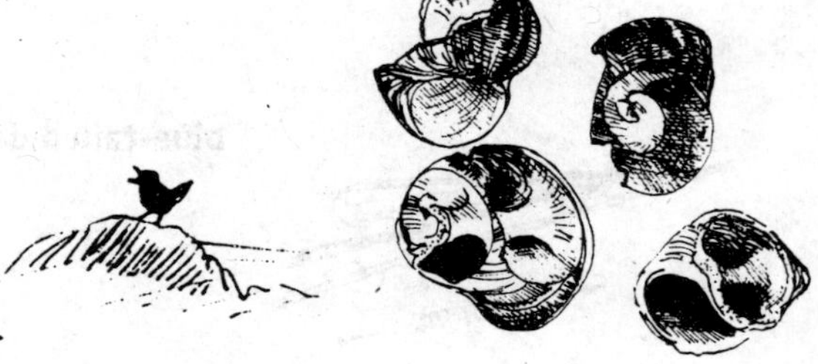

more s.b.j.'s

If you sit quietly in the seemingly empty moorland, you'll begin to notice little birds flitting over the heather: trouble is, they're all S.B.J.'s! Take the two sorts of **pipit**.

meadow pipit longer tail and beak, flesh-coloured legs.

rock pipit usually only found near coast. Darker with dark legs.

Think of them as rocket and mipit and at least you might feel less confused…

Then there are the chats – which say 'chat' or 'chack', like two pebbles tapped together.

wheatear: white rump, very obvious in flight, black bandit mask

stonechat: seen close up, far from brown: the male has a black head, white neckband and russet breast. Perches very upright.

MAKE A DRAGONFLY

YOU NEED:

- Two 30 cm lengths of strong, bendable wire
- Two coloured pipe cleaners
- Two medium sized beads with large holes (e.g. hair beads)
- Scraps of cellophane

1. Attach the beads by threading them through each pipe cleaner and wrapping the ends back on themselves.

2. To finish making the body, twist the pipe cleaners together. The beads make up the dragonfly's eyes.

3. Make two sets of wings by bending each piece of wire into a double set. Leave spare wire in the middle. Wrap each wing with cellophane or cover with sellotape and colour in with indelible felt pens.

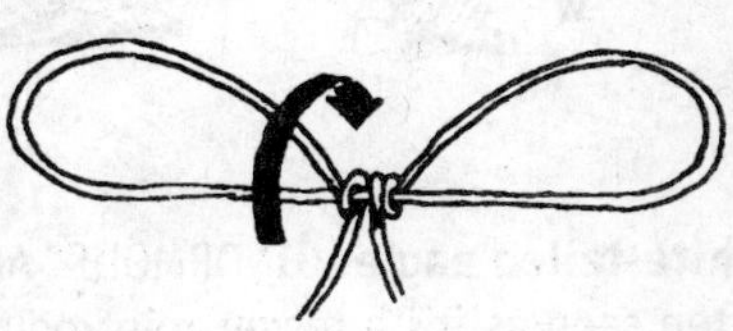

4. Wrap the loose wire from middle of wings firmly around the body, a quarter of the way along from the eyes to complete your dragonfly.

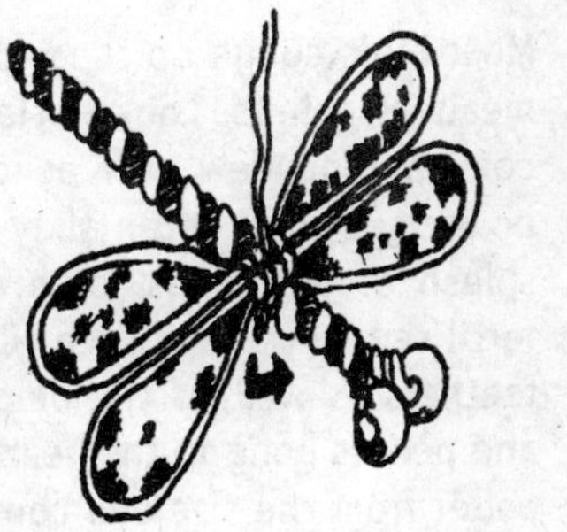

raptor roundup

Sit around for a while and you might see some **raptor** action. Raptors are hunters – birds of prey.

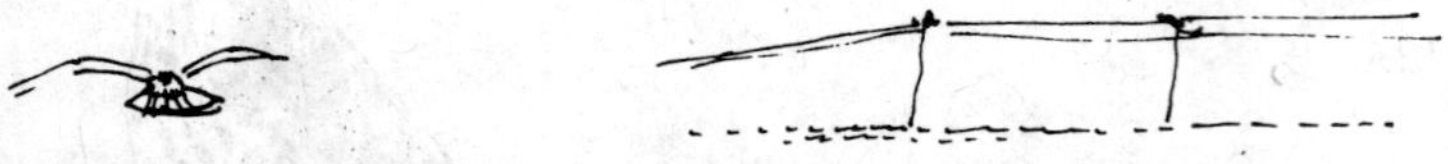

kestrel: (uncommon in Lewis and Harris) pale underneath, hovers almost motionless, pounces on small birds, rodents and insects.

merlin: small, dark, very fast falcon, tears in low after small birds, twisting and turning with incredible agility as they try to escape. Nests in trees if there are any, otherwise in bushy heather with a good view of SBJ-land below.

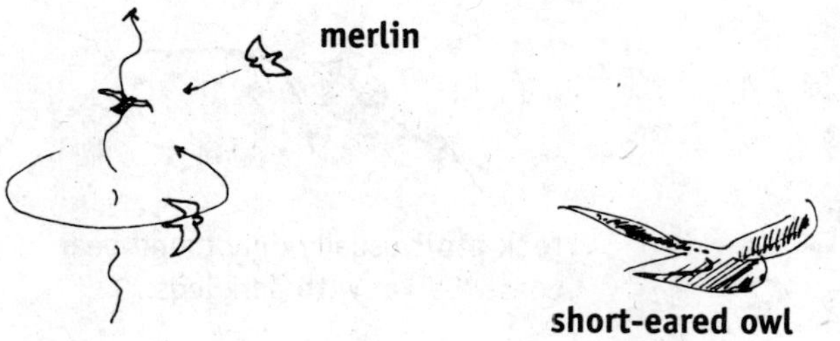

peregrine (not illustrated here): our largest falcon, a magnificent flyer which strikes larger birds such as rock doves, redshanks and snipe in the air. It nests on sea or mountain cliffs, but hunts over moorland as well.

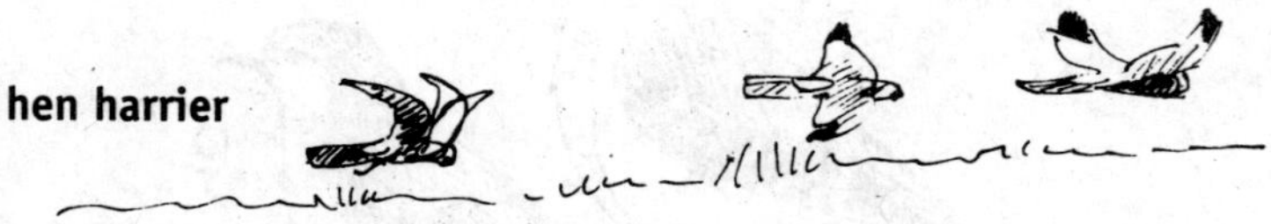

hen harrier: look for dark wingtips. Not found in Lewis and Harris, because it's more of a vole-harrier really (Gaelic name <u>clamhan-luch</u> means that!) and like the **short-eared owl** lives in the Uists, where there are plenty voles.

buzzard: BIG. Shorter neck and more rounded wings distinguish it from the eagle. Different habits too- visits croftland and coast as well as moorland, anywhere with rabbits. Often perches on fenceposts. Eagles only do this when they are very young and foolish.

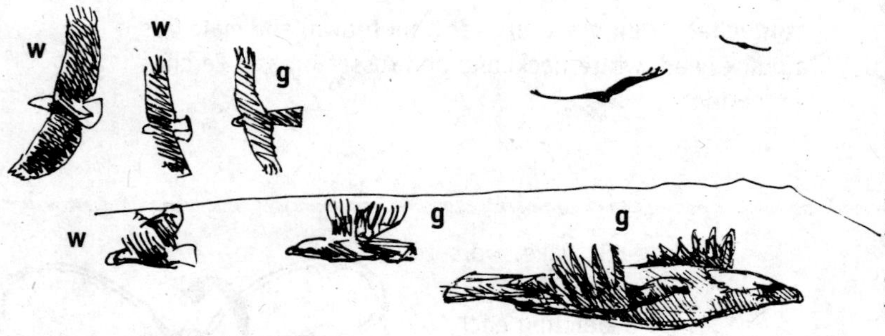

golden eagle: BIGGER. Magnificent mountain bird, quartering a huge territory in immensely powerful flight. The golden feathers on the neck are only visible from above. Hunts rabbits, grouse etc, and also takes carrion.

white-tailed eagle: GINORMOUS. Amazingly so. Not often seen as it's a recent reintroduction and there are very few around. Eats seabirds and fish but hunts coastal moorland too.

Most birds cough up the indigestible parts of their meals as pellets. Look for favourite perches with a commanding view, such as lone boulders, old walls, or rocky bluffs. Often they are detectable from a splash of droppings, or a cap of lichen or moss fertilised by years of such whitewash. There may be feathers as well, if the perch is used by a raptor, and pellets lying in the heather. You can tell whose pellet from the size and contents.

merlin: about 4 x 2cm, well stuck together, containing downy underfeathers of small birds, sometimes iridescent beetle wing cases.
peregrine: about 5 x 3cm, underfeathers of waders, maybe small fragments of bone.
hooded crow: about 5 x 2cm, with pointed ends, insect remains, seeds and sheep wool.
short-eared owl: about 6 x 2cm, long and light, always containing recognisable rodent remains.
herring gull: about 3 x 2 cm, loose, dry pellets which disintegrate quickly, containing shells of molluscs and crustaceans (eg crabs).

NB pellets are not collectibles – and you should finish your crisps before you investigate them!

Raptors don't much like each other and ravens don't like any of them. Although they take different prey species, all these birds use the same terrain and defend large hunting territories to feed their families. So when you're tired of trying to sort out the S.B.J's, scan the skies, and you may have the good luck to witness one of their frequent tussles – a pair of furious peregrines shrieking at a buzzard, or a family of ravens confusing a soaring eagle with nimble aerobatics, even tweaking the intruder's wings!

all about peat

But what is this soggy brown PEAT stuff anyway? It's the remains of ancient vegetation, mostly of **sphagnum moss**. Sphagnum is the soft, springy moss which paints peatlands many colours – varying from almost white when dry, through shades of green and yellow, and even red. It acts like a sponge, so water that would otherwise run off or form pools collects in the moss and the ground under it remains wet – just like the side of the bath does if you leave an unsqueezed sponge on it.

Sphagnum can hold up to twenty times its weight in water. Because it's so absorbent, it was used in the days before nappies to line babies' cradles. It was also used in the First World War for dressing wounds.

There's a story that the islands once had forests, and that it was burning and pillaging Vikings who destroyed them. This isn't exactly what the peat tells us. There were certainly more trees when humans first came to the islands, mostly scrubby birch and hazel, much of which was probably gradually cut for fuel or cleared for agriculture. There were forests of larger trees in at least two places, Airidhbhruaich in Lewis and on ground now covered by sea off Pabbay, in the Sound of Harris. Apparently there was never anything like total forest cover: areas like central Lewis have pure peat down to the glacial till left after the Ice Age. However, woodland probably did well during the Viking period – not because Norsemen were into saving trees, but because this was a period when the climate was warmer and drier than today. After that there followed a cooler spell, and trees have never had such a good chance since, so if you put two and two together and don't like Vikings, you might conclude the lack of trees was their fault. Grazing has probably had a far greater effect than burning and pillaging.

In a warmer or dryer climate dead vegetation soon decomposes into soil, but in cool wet conditions, the ground may be so waterlogged that air doesn't get into it, so microbes can't get to work on it, so the organic material doesn't rot. The softer fragments are compressed by the sheer weight of new layers and harder items like wood are preserved. Grains of pollen are tiny but hard, so they too are preserved in the peat. Scientists use radiocarbon dating to decide when the peat was formed. They can then tell what plants were around at the time from examining the pollen record.

Tree is craobh in Gaelic. Oak, rowan, willow and alder are darrach, caorann, seileach and fearna. Look on Ordnance Survey maps and see if you can find any 'tree' placenames (they might be spelt differently, though). Are there still trees there today?

Peat is almost 90% water! When cut for fuel, the slabs are at first very heavy, soggy and breakable, but when sun and wind have dried them for a few weeks, they become tough, light and of course a lot smaller. In the old 'blackhouses', the peat fire was in the middle of the room and there was no chimney – that's why the house was black, from the smoke filtering its way through the thatch. Every few years the smokey thatch was replaced, and the old thatch was used as compost. Just one example of how everything was recycled. There's a Blackhouse Museum at Arnol in Lewis.

wet, wetter, unbelievably wet

Peat forms wherever plants have grown in cool, wet conditions.

Peat moorland is found on hilly ground. The peat covering may be quite thin. On the hilltops, and in the Bays area in east Harris, there's as much bare rock as peat. There are boggy pockets between the rock, with some lochans. This is the terrain where you are most likely to see raptors. Look out too for divers flying overhead. The most common is the **red-throated diver**, but even it is a rare and threatened species.

NB Divers are very shy birds and hatch only one chick a year. It is illegal to disturb them (as well as unkind) so be very careful not to go near if you think they are nesting.

Valley bog forms wetter peat where hills drain down to the bog on either side, and long channels or streams may form. This sort of mountain-and-bog terrain is common in south Lewis, Harris and North Uist. Look up and you may see **red deer**. They're so well camouflaged against the hillside vegetation you probably won't notice them till they move. More surprisingly, in this grand, wild setting, you'll often hear the song of **blackbird** and **thrush** echoing across the valleys. With the steady supply of invertebrate life available in wet ground, and plenty rock crevices to nest in, they're as much at home here as in a town garden.

Blanket bog speaks for itself, doesn't it? The flat interior of Lewis and Benbecula are prime examples. Deep, even peat with many lochans of all sizes. This is real bog enthusiasts' bog, and it's now recognised as INTERNATIONALLY IMPORTANT – must be nice for it after all these centuries of being just smelly old bog...

How many deer can you see?

Wherever you go between coast and coast in the islands, there's water! In fact, if you fly over Benbecula and the Uists, there seems to be more water than land.

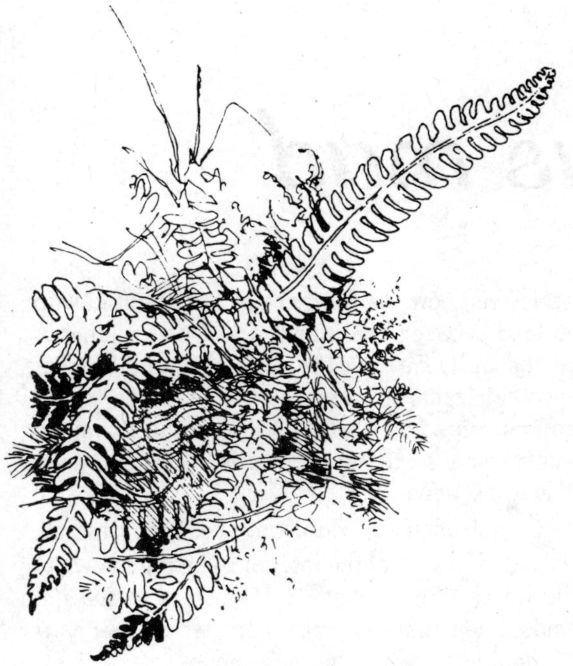

In summer, nearly every loch has a fiddler! The Gaelic name of the **common sandpiper** is fidhleir bòrd-an-locha, the fiddler by the loch. You'll see him bobbing a white tail at the water's edge, calling 'fiddle-de-dee, fiddle-de-dee, fiddle-de-dee, fiddle-de-dee'.

Only a limited range of plants can survive the very acid peat. The mixture varies according to the degree of wetness. Look on bare areas of wet black peat for **viviparous fescue**. 'Viviparous' means 'bearing live young'. This grass forms plantlets at the end of the blades, which take root in their turn. In drier areas you may find **crowberry**, which looks like a heather but isn't: its berries are much valued by small birds. It stains their droppings bright purple – look for the tell-tale splashes in July and August. Peaty lochans often hold the beautiful **white waterlily**. Look too for lichens – even if you have never seen them before, you'll recognise **woolly fringe moss** and **fairies' matches** from their names.

Small islands in lochs can't be reached by grazing animals, or by the muirburn fires that people have used for centuries to encourage young short growth for their flocks. So they often have a luxuriant cap of shrub vegetation, bright green in summer against the dark peatland. Look out for **grey herons** which nest on some larger loch islands. **Rowan**, with its flat heads of creamy blossom followed by scarlet berries, is one of the commonest trees, with **willow, alder, wild rose, bramble, honeysuckle** and **blaeberry.** But probably nothing will be over a metre or two high! It's a forest on an elfin scale. As in taller forests, the trees affect local conditions, breaking the force of wind and rain, protecting the ground from both waterlogging and drying out, and adding humus which encourages invertebrate life. These islets have their own microclimate, milder and calmer than the moorland, and support ferns, lichens and mosses, and particularly delicate liverworts, which don't thrive in the open.

Once you start thinking in terms of microclimate, you realise that tree-grown islands aren't the only places with distinct conditions. Sheltered crevices under broken rocks and even old bushy heather also moderate the excesses of bad weather. Then rock may retain the sun's warmth, or stay permanently cold in a shady position with dripping water. Different microclimates with different vegetation (and so a whole different ecosystem) may coexist within a few metres. Microclimate means microhabitat.

Explore a **micro nature trail**! Take a piece of thin string a metre long, and wind it round 'features' (like ferns or pebbles) in your chosen nook or cranny. Inspect closely – a magnifying glass and a bug box will make this more fun.

DINERS AND DINNERS – pair them all up

midge larva
sundew
tick
crowberry
midge
vole
merlin
sheep blood
dragonfly
meadow pipit
twite
shorteared owl

Peatlands aren't so boring after all!

6. Glorious mud

On the east coast of the islands, you'll find a positive jumble of hard and soft shore, but the soft bits are mud rather than the sand found on the West.

mud stinks!

That's because it contains a lot of organic material, like seaweed and plankton, which rots down gently in places where there are no big waves to sweep it away. This means the mud and the tides which rise and fall gently over it are full of nourishment. A dense community of burrowers thrives under the mud. As in sandy shores there are bivalves, gastropods and worms, but they are different species, which have adapted to cope with a sticky, clogging environment. The most common are:

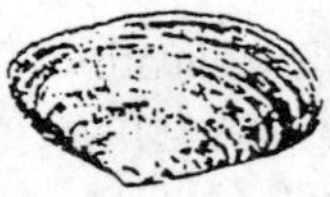

baltic tellin, bivalve, sturdy, rounded pink or yellow shell, 1 – 2cm

peppery furrow shell, bivalve, light brownish cream, darker round edge of 'gape', 5 – 6cm. Leaves star-shaped marks on the mud when it draws in its siphon.

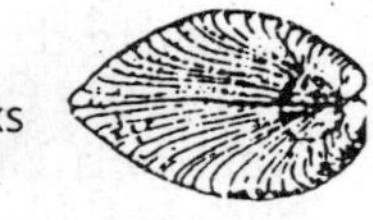

hydrobia, gastropod, with white, tiny five or six-whorled spire shell (1mm upwards)

ragworm, yellowish-brown with red line down back, 9 – 12cm. Look for casts – you're unlikely to see the worm except if a bird pulls one out while you are watching.

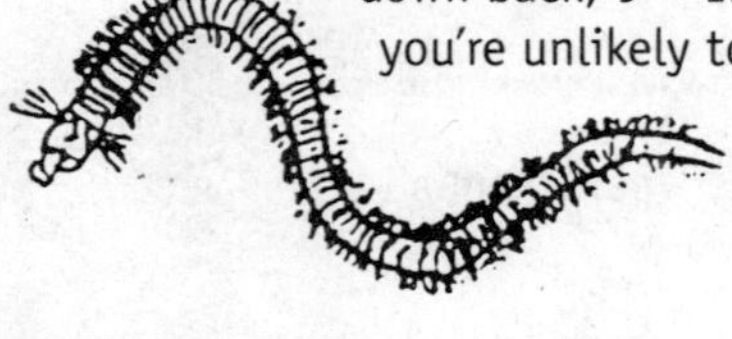

sandhopper (1 – 1.5 cm) lives in U-shaped burrows between tidelines – you'll see the thousands of 2mm holes on the surface, more often than the hoppers.

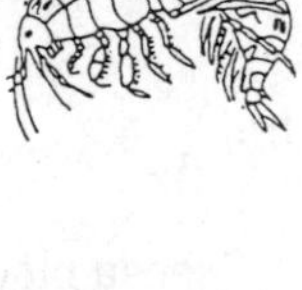

Low tide is a great time for human beachcombers as well as for wildlife. But remember this is the birds' best chance to feed. Noise, sudden movements and bright colours will drive them away. If you're considerate, you'll see more wildlife anyway.

We've seen how the full force of the Atlantic, with no land between the islands and America, pounds on the west, creating the vast shell sand beaches and the machair. The sea on the east side is very different: it's from the Atlantic that the prevailing winds come, so the east coast is sheltered by the land in between.

So – no breakers, no shifting shell sand. Instead, the rock and peat of the interior come right down to the water. Over thousands of years, the sea has gradually eaten its way into the softer or lower parts of the land, leaving the rocky bones intact. There are many tiny bays and islands and long sealochs snake inland. Some of these lochs, Seaforth for example, are very deep, but the sea enters over a shallow 'sill', so that the upper layers of water move faster than the bottom, and this ecosystem supports rich marine life with species that can only survive in calm but deep water, such as the **sea-pen**. Others such as Lochmaddy have creeks which are only entered by the sea at very high tides, so they are brackish – less salty than seawater – and this too produces a very special ecosystem. Freshwater and saltwater species exist side by side, together with some particular to brackish water. These conditions produce plenty of food for waterfowl.

The children of Cliasmol school did a special study of seaweed for their wildlife competition entry, including finding out about its uses – for example, it is used in the food-processing industry as a gelling agent for desserts and ice cream.

danger!

Be VERY CAREFUL on rocks near the water. They're slippery, and also it's easy to mistake floating weed for a firm foothold. Kelp is a very tall weed growing in deep water – don't be fooled by its broad strap-like brown fronds showing above the surface, it's a LONG WAY DOWN.

weedy world

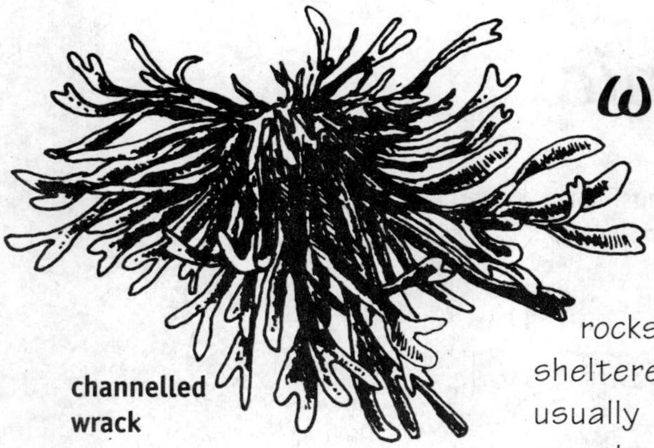

channelled wrack

Over-hanging rocks in these sheltered bays usually have a covering of long seaweed. There's a whole new colourful world under the veil. If you lift the weed carefully, there will probably be a sudden scuttle – escaping hoppers and small **shore crabs**. The other rock residents aren't so flighty – the rock may well contain a clump of blue black **common mussels**. These are filter-feeding bivalves which live between the tidelines. They anchor themselves firmly to the rocks and to each other by means of their fibrous <u>byssus</u> – the 'beard'. Emerald green **sea grapes**, yellow and orange **starsquirts**, light green **breadcrumb sponge** looking like a collection of little volcanoes, blue **winkles** and crimson **beadlet anemones** cling to the rock and lodge in the crevices. In the weed itself you'll find grazing **periwinkles**, olive green, yellow, orange or striped like a mint humbug. The vivid crimson and pink **topshell** belongs to another grazing snail.

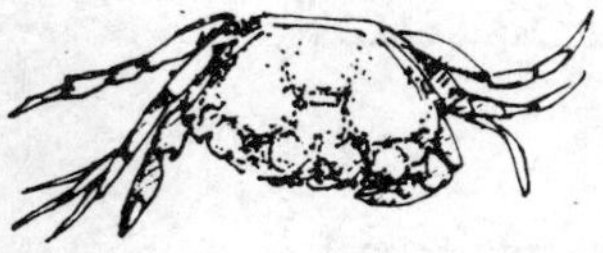

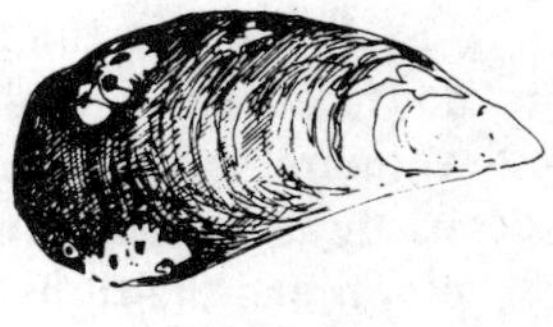

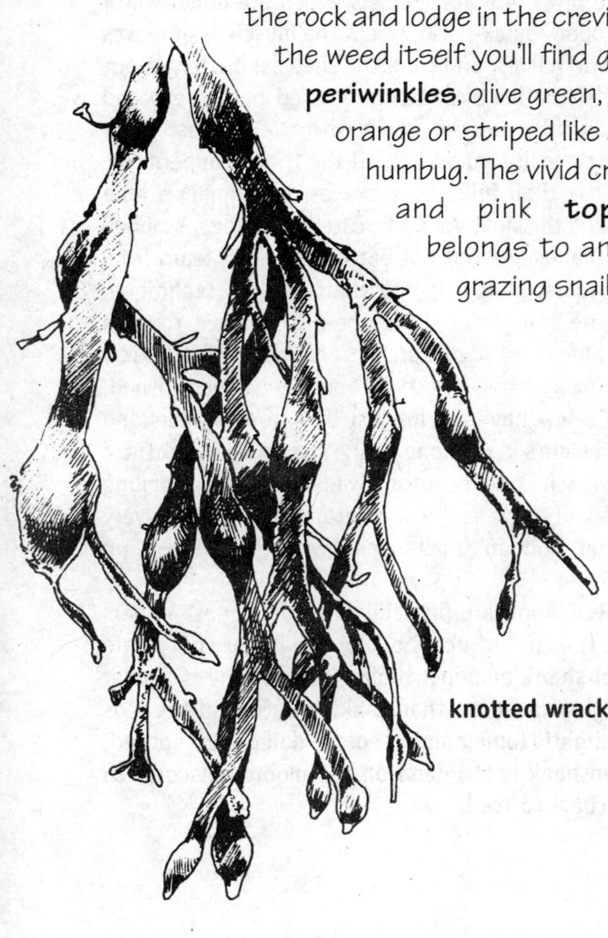

knotted wrack

bladder wrack

Seaweeds are algae, not 'weeds'. They don't have roots or flowers. They anchor themselves against being washed away by means of a <u>holdfast</u> to rocks, other weeds, or shells. There are green, brown and red seaweeds. Look for bright green **sea lettuce** at the top of the shore, especially where there's fresh water running down. The short yellowy brown **channelled wrack** grows in the intertidal zone. Dark brown **bladder wrack** and **knotted wrack** form the veils on middle shore boulders with **toothed wrack** slightly lower down. All wracks have air-filled bladders to keep them afloat – the things it's fun to pop, but don't overdo it and spoil the lifejacket! Below the low tide level are the brown flat fronds of **kelp**. The red seaweeds are mostly small and delicate and often hidden under other weed at or below low tide. Look for **dulse**, with short, shiny flat red fronds that have a gleam of purple. It's quite crisp and tasty. No seaweeds are poisonous, so it's safe to experiment, but most are very tough!

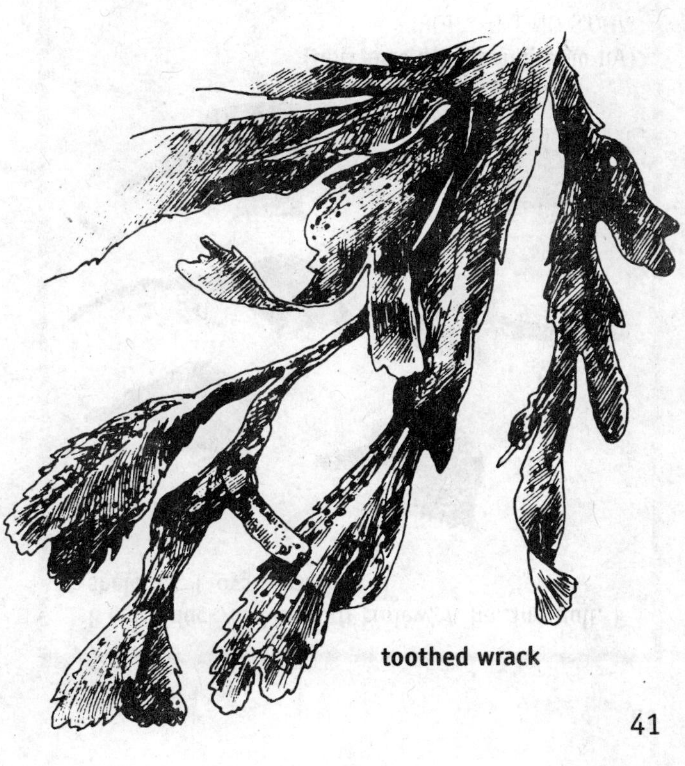

toothed wrack

waders' picnic

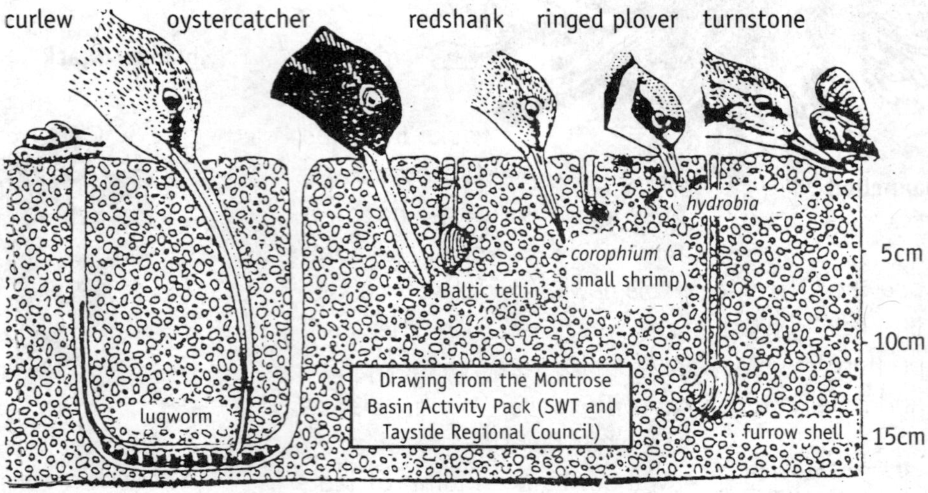

Drawing from the Montrose Basin Activity Pack (SWT and Tayside Regional Council)

Mud-and-rock shoreline provides a banquet for waders. The smaller species, redshank, dunlin and ringed plover for example, probe the mud for the burrowers. Larger birds, such as curlew and oystercatchers, also take larger prey from the rocks. The different birds don't compete too much because, although they all feed on the same patch of mud, their different lengths and types of beaks mean they can reach prey at different depths. Leg length is important too, as the longer-legged birds can wade deeper and take prey while the water is still covering the mud.

It's not only a waders' feast. All sorts of gulls come too. Black-headed gulls (and sometimes herring gulls) have an interesting feeding technique: they wade in shallow water, stand on one spot and trample like mad! The suction caused by their flat, webbed feet brings prey to the surface. Waders sometimes hang about to pick up the remains. See if you can spot this happening

WHO'S ON THE SHORE?
(All mentioned in this section)

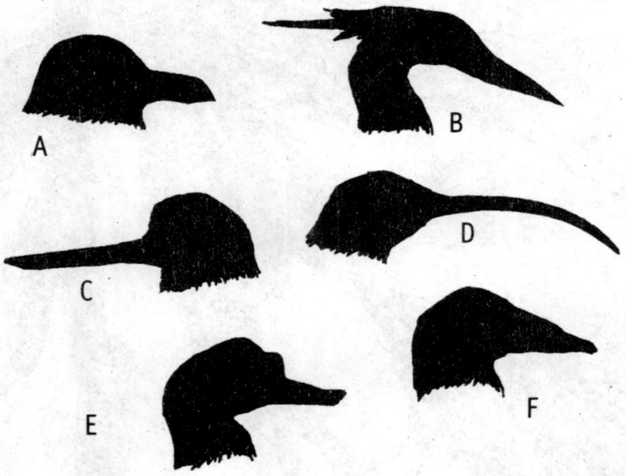

F eider duck, B heron, D curlew, A herring gull, E shelduck, C oystercatcher.

Just to confuse things, a long bill and long legs don't *necessarily* mean a prober in deep water! The **whimbrel** is long in both bill and legs, yet it feeds mostly at the strand line, with the short-billed **ringed plover** and the **turnstone**, which is a flicker, not a prober at all. What's important to avoid head-on competition is that each species has a different feeding technique, in which length of legs and length and type of bill play their part.

Oystercatchers have long, very strong bills, which they use to force open mussels, which can close very tightly. There are two ways of doing this. Some birds look for mussels which are under water and open, quickly stab to cut the muscle that closes the two halves, and carry the shell ashore to get out the flesh. Other birds pick out closed mussels exposed by the tide, position them with the weakest point (on the inside curve behind the hinge) uppermost, and use their bills like pickaxes, to hammer a hole through the shell. An oystercatcher may be a 'stabber' or a 'hammerer' but not both. The chicks learn from their parents by copying their feeding technique, and are brought up to do one or the other. You can tell which sort of oystercatcher has been feeding by looking at the empty shells after they have finished.

Curlew have the longest bills of all waders and the female's is still longer: she can probe down 15cm and reach food no other wader can. Look among flocks of curlews for a solitary **whimbrel** – very similar, though smaller, and with dark stripes on the head.

Redshank are probably the commonest waders on the mud, but occasionally you might spot a rare **greenshank** amongst them. The plumage is similar but greyish rather than pinkish buff, and the legs are slightly longer and of course dull green, not red. Greenshank nest inland on the moors but come to the coast to feed.

cunning corvids

You may be surprised to see **hooded crows** pecking around with the shore birds. Crows are great scavengers, and always on the lookout for things to steal from other birds, but they also have a special feeding technique of their own. Hoodies crack their mussels by dropping them from a height onto a rock, often repeating the trick time and time again until the shell breaks. It's quite a skill getting the height right – too low and it doesn't crack, too high and another crow may get their first...

The hooded crow, mostly grey with black 'hood', wings and tail, replaces the all-black carrion crow in the west. The all-black corvid common in the islands is the much larger **raven** – magnificently black all over, beak, legs and all. In late summer you often see 'clans' of ravens enjoying themselves free-falling, rolling and looping the loop together. Like hoodies, they're not above scavenging the shore line, particularly if anything dead is washed up.

Corvids (crow family) are highly intelligent, long-lived opportunistic birds. Odin, king of the Norse gods, had two pet ravens, Hugin and Munin (Forethought and Memory) who ranged the world every day to pick up all the news, and came back each evening to keep Odin informed of what was going on down below. There is a tradition in Britain that ravens are always kept at the Tower of London: if they die out, it's supposed to herald the downfall of the realm. In 1995, two young ravens from Uist went on duty at the Tower. They were named after Odin's ravens.

MUD GAME – CURLEWS AND TURNSTONES

YOU NEED:
a tube of Smarties
2 dice
a plate
plastic straws and cups

1. Divide Smarties – half in a cup, and half on a plate with an upturned cup over them. Set both lots at the 'low tide line'.
2. 2 teams – curlews and turnstones – line up behind the 'high tide line', each team with a dice. Each player gets a 'beak' (a straw) and a cup to put the 'catch' in.
3. Players take it in turns to shake dice. When a six is thrown, curlews run to the cup at 'low tide' and suck Smarties up – beak only, no hands! – dropping the 'catch' into their own cup. Turnstones do the same with the plate of Smarties – flicking the upturned cup off first with the 'beak'.
4. Each time another six is thrown, a new player takes over the correct food supply. N.B. Turnstones replace upturned cup before leaving – hands allowed for this!

Winners are the first team to pick up all their Smarties.

family fun

Herons on the islands have to nest where they can find trees or shrub-covered ledges, and these may not be ideal places to teach the young birds to fish. So parents often bring the youngsters somewhere with calm water and a guaranteed supply of fish. During August and September, you can watch them learning the knack of standing quite still and catching eels and fish with a lightning stab.

The sheltered mud-and-rock inlets with their plentiful food and calm water are nurseries for a number of young families. **Eider duck, mallard** and **red-breasted merganser** ducklings often take their first swim here, following Mum in a tight cheeping huddle. If danger threatens, the brown ducklings get some camouflage from brown seaweed floating around the rocks. **Shelduck** parents both share in bringing up the babies, and since mud is where they find their favourite food, hydrobia, you may well see family groups. Or you may just find their webbed footprints and the curious 'scything' marks made by their flat, slightly upturned bills on the mud, as they sieve out the tiny snails.

Otter mothers have to teach their cubs (from one to three of them, usually two) to hunt. In the Western Isles otters do most of their fishing in the sea, but rough waves are dangerous for cubs, and they also need access to fresh water. So a sheltered bay with a stream running into it is ideal. The cubs have to learn to deal with wriggling, flapping fish (usually **butterfish** or **lumpfish**, found under rocks in shallow water). Their mother brings a live one ashore, and they have to kill it before they get any dinner – not easy at first! Young cubs don't like the water – Mum has to coax or even nudge them in – but soon they become very active and playful. One of the highlights of wildlife watching is the sight of an otter family swimming together, or tumbling and sliding down seaweedy rocks. They'll do this again and again, even when grown up! Families stay together until the cubs are as big as the mother.

raven's eye view

Now you have explored the islands from coast to coast – from the sandy Atlantic beaches, through the machair, to the peatlands, boggy or hilly, of the interior, and down to the sheltered rock and mud sea-inlets on the Minch side.

One of the nice things about being on an island is that you can climb almost any hill and have that raven's eye view. Try it, after you've visited all the habitats in this book.

If you *were* a raven, and could swoop anywhere you wanted in minutes, where would you most like to go? What if you were a goose, hungry for green pasture after a long flight from the Arctic, or a corncrake returning after a winter in Africa looking for a mate? A merlin fancying a bite of twite? Which habitat would suit you?

Can you mark these habitats on the section below? Sea, sand, machair and loch, croftland, moorland, hill, peaty loch, mud/rocky shore, sea

Does everything make more sense?

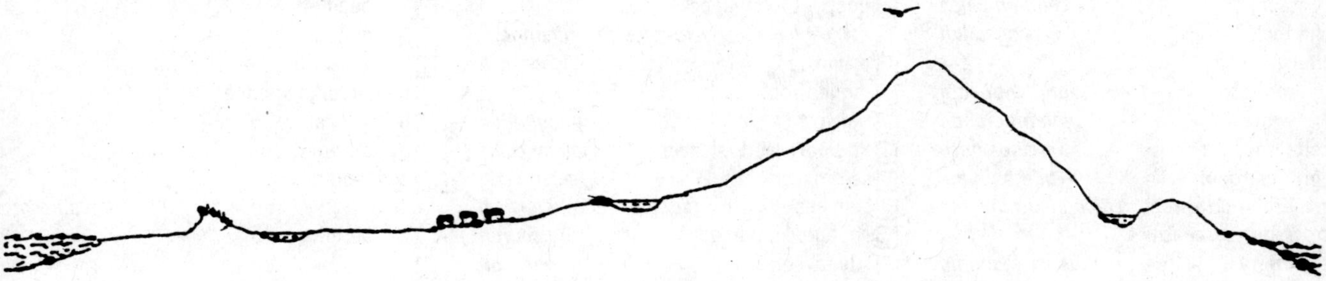

useful books

Inexpensive and compact series of field-guides are:

Collins Pocket Guides, especially *Wild Flowers of Britain and Europe*

Collins Gem Guides, especially the *Gem Guide to the Seashore*

Mitchell Beazley Pocket Guides, especially the *Birdwatcher's Pocket Guide* and *Butterflies of Britain and Europe*

Don't be without:

Peter Cunningham *Birds of the Outer Hebrides: their status and distribution*, Mercat Press, ISBN 0901824992

Other useful guides are:

Lars Jonsson *Birds of Europe*, Helm, ISBN 0713644222

A.C. Campbell *The Country Life Guide to the Seashore and Shallow Seas of Britain and Europe*, Country Life, ISBN 0600343960

B. Skinner *Colour Identification Guide to Moths of the British Isles*, Viking, ISBN 0670803545

Michael Chinery *Field Guide to the Insects of Britain and Northern Europe*, Collins, ISBN 002191377

Cyril Hammond and Robert Merritt *Dragonflies of Great Britain and Ireland*, 2nd edition, Harley Books, ISBN 0946589143

And if you enjoy a peep into the past:

William MacGillivray, edited by R. Ralph *A Hebridean Naturalist's Journal, 1817–1818*, Acair Press, ISBN 0861521226

Check lists

These lists include most (not all) of the birds, mammals and flowers you are likely to see in the Western Isles, and a small selection of other interesting things. You can tick as you see them, or keep your own lists in your field notebook. If you live in the islands you could add Gaelic names where there are gaps we couldn't fill. Ask friends and relatives, particularly older people.
Don't be disappointed if you see far fewer species than are listed – just enjoy whatever you do see, and keep your eyes and ears open!

FLOWERING PLANTS

- ☐ alkanet *bog-lus*
- ☐ amphibious bistort *glùineach an uisge*
- ☐ autumn hawkbit
- ☐ bartsia, red
- bedstraw
  - ☐ heath *màdar fraoich*
  - ☐ lady's *lus an leasaich*
- ☐ bird's foot trefoil *barra-mhislean*
- ☐ bog asphodel
- ☐ bog pimpernel *falcair lèana*
- ☐ bogbean *tri-bhileach*
- ☐ buttercup *buideachan t-samhraidh*
- ☐ centaury *ceud-bhileach*
- ☐ charlock *sgeallan*
- clovers
  - ☐ red *seamrag dhearg*
  - ☐ white *seamhrag bhàn*
- ☐ coltsfoot *cluas liath*
- ☐ corn marigold *bile bhuidhe*
- ☐ cranesbill, dovesfoot *croba preachain mìn*
- ☐ cross-leaved heath
- ☐ crowberry *lus na feannaig*
- ☐ cuckoo flower *flur na cuthaig*
- ☐ daisy *neoinean*
- ☐ dandelion *beàrnan brìde*
- dead-nettle
  - ☐ red *deanntag dhearg*
  - ☐ white *deanntag bhàn*
- ☐ dog violet *dail-chuaich*
- ☐ eyebright *lus nan leac*
- ☐ field gentian *lus a' chrùbain*
- ☐ flag iris *sealasdair*
- ☐ forget me not *lus midhe aitich*
- ☐ foxglove *lus nam ban-sidh*
- ☐ harebell (Scottish bluebell)
- heather
  - ☐ bell *fraoch a' bhadain*
  - ☐ ling *fraoch*
- ☐ hogweed
- ☐ honeysuckle *iadh-shlat*
- ☐ kidney vetch
- ☐ kingcup *lus buidhe bealtainn*
- ☐ knapweed *cnapan dubh*
- ☐ lady's bedstraw
- ☐ lesser meadow-rue
- ☐ lousewort *lus riabhach monaidh*
- ☐ marsh cinquefoil *coig-bhileach uisge*
- ☐ mayweed *buidheag an arbhair*
- ☐ meadowsweet *cneas chù-chulainn*
- ☐ milkwort *lus a' bhainne*
- ☐ mountain everlasting *spòg cait*
- ☐ mugwort
- orchid
  - ☐ butterfly *mogairlean an dean-dè mor*
  - ☐ common spotted
  - ☐ early marsh *mogairlean lèana*
  - ☐ frog *mogairlean lusgainn*
  - ☐ Hebridean *urach-bhallach*
  - ☐ heath spotted *mogairleann mointich*
  - ☐ northern marsh *mogairlean purpaidh*
- ☐ pansy, wild *goirmean-searradh*
- ☐ pennywort *lus na peighinn*
- ☐ pondweed *lìobhag*
- ☐ poppy, longheaded *crom-lus fad-cheannach*
- ☐ primrose *sobhrach*
- ☐ ragged robin
- ☐ ragwort *buaghallan*
- ☐ St John's wort, slender *lus chaluim chille*
- ☐ sea rocket *fearsaideag*
- ☐ self-heal *dubhan ceann-chòsach*
- ☐ shepherd's purse *an sporan*
- ☐ silverweed *brisgean*
- ☐ sorrel *sealbhag*
- ☐ spearwort
- speedwell
  - ☐ germander *nuallach*
  - ☐ water *fualachdar*
- ☐ spring squill *leat-uinnean*
- stonecrop
  - ☐ English *biadh an t-sionnadh*
  - ☐ biting *grabhan nan clach*
- ☐ storksbill, common *gob corra*
- sundew
  - ☐ great *lus a'ghadmainn*
  - ☐ oblong-leaved *dealt ruaidhe*
  - ☐ round-leaved *lus na feàrnaich*
- ☐ thistle *cluaran*
- ☐ thrift *tonn a'cladaich*
- ☐ thyme *lus na macraidh, lus an rìgh*
- ☐ tormentil *cairt lair*
- ☐ twayblade
- ☐ vetch, common *peasair, chapaill*
- ☐ water avens *machall uisge*
- ☐ water lobelia *flùr an lochan*
- ☐ water mint *meannt an usige*
- ☐ white waterlily *duilleag-bhaite bhàn*
- ☐ wild carrot *curran talmhainn*
- ☐ yarrow *eàrr thalmhainn*
- ☐ yellow rattle *modhalan buidhe*

GRASSES

- ☐ bog cotton *canach*
- ☐ deer grass *cìob, ultanaich*
- fescue
  - ☐ red *fèisd ruadh*
  - ☐ viviparous
- ☐ marram grass *muran*
- ☐ purple moor grass *fianach*
- ☐ quaking grass *conan cumant*
- ☐ Yorkshire fog *feur a chinn bhàin*

SHORE FINDS

- anemone
  - ☐ beadlet
  - ☐ dhalia
  - ☐ snakelocks
- ☐ breadcrumb sponge
- ☐ brittle star
- ☐ by-the-wind sailor
- ☐ common starfish
- crab *partan*
  - ☐ hermit
  - ☐ shore
- ☐ dab
- ☐ goby
- ☐ hydrobia
- ☐ jellyfish
- ☐ lugworm
- ☐ mermaid's purse
- ☐ pea urchin
- ☐ ragworm
- ☐ sandeel
- ☐ sand hopper
- ☐ sand mason
- ☐ sea potato
- ☐ sea urchin
- ☐ seabean
- ☐ sea slater
- ☐ sea slug
- ☐ shrimp *carran*
- ☐ starsquirt
- ☐ sunstar

SHELLS

- ☐ banded wedge shell
- ☐ cockle
- ☐ common artemis
- ☐ cowrie
- ☐ dog cockle
- ☐ dog whelk
- ☐ Iceland clam

limpet *bàirneach*
- ☐ blue-rayed
- ☐ common
- ☐ keyhole
- ☐ slipper

☐ mussel *feusgan*
☐ necklace shell
☐ otter shell
☐ pelican's foot
☐ peppery furrow shell
☐ periwinkle
☐ razorshell

scallop
- ☐ common *slige-chreachainn*
- ☐ tiger
- ☐ queen

☐ sting winkle
☐ sunset shell

tellin
- ☐ baltic
- ☐ thin

topshell
- ☐ common
- ☐ painted

☐ tower shell
☐ warty venus
☐ whelk *màigh dealag*
☐ winkle

SEAWEEDS

☐ bootlace weed
☐ carrageen
☐ dulse
☐ kelp
☐ maerl
☐ sea lettuce

wrack *bristeadh, sgrios*
- ☐ bladder
- ☐ channelled
- ☐ knotted
- ☐ toothed

BUGS

butterfly
- ☐ common blue *dealan gorm*
- ☐ dark green fritillary
- ☐ green-veined white
- ☐ large heath
- ☐ large white *dealan a'chail*
- ☐ meadow brown dealan donn
- ☐ painted lady
- ☐ red admiral
- ☐ small heath
- ☐ small white
- ☐ small tortoiseshell *dealan breac-bhallach*

☐ cranefly (daddy longlegs) *fidhlear*

damselfly
- ☐ blue-tailed *tarbh-nathrach gorm*
- ☐ common blue
- ☐ large red

dragonfly
- ☐ black darter
- ☐ four-spotted chaser
- ☐ highland darter
- ☐ common hawker

☐ dung beetle *ceardaman*
☐ dungfly
☐ ground beetle *cearran cre*
☐ Hebridean bumble bee *seillean mor*
☐ midge *meanbh-chuileag*

moth *leòman, raodan, cnuimh*
- ☐ angle shades
- ☐ cinnabar
- ☐ emperor
- ☐ Hebrew character
- ☐ puss

☐ water boatman
☐ water scorpion

MAMMALS

☐ brown rat *radan*
☐ field vole *buaidh-iomlan*
☐ hare *maigheach, gearr*
☐ hedgehog *cràineag*
☐ mink
☐ mouse *luch*
☐ otter *dòbhran*
☐ polecat *feòcullan, taghan*
☐ shrew *té ladarna, bancheard*
☐ rabbit *coinean*
☐ red deer *fiadh*

seal *ròn, comharradh*
- ☐ common
- ☐ grey

CETACEANS

dolphin *an leumadair*
- ☐ bottlenose
- ☐ common
- ☐ Risso's
- ☐ whitebeaked
- ☐ whitesided

☐ porpoise *péileag*

whale *muc-mhara*
- ☐ killer
- ☐ minke
- ☐ pilot

BIRDS

☐ black guillemot *gerra-breac*
☐ blackbird *l'on-dubh*
☐ blackcap *cean dubh*
☐ buzzard *clamhan*

bunting
- ☐ corn *gealag bhuchair*
- ☐ reed *gealag loin*

☐ chaffinch
☐ coot *luch bhlair*
☐ cormorant *sgarbh*
☐ corncrake *traon*
☐ curlew *guilbneach*
☐ dabchick (little grebe) *spàg-ri-ton*
☐ dunlin *gille-feadaig*
☐ eider duck *lach lochlannach*
☐ fulmar *fulmair, eun-crom*
☐ gannet *sulaire*
☐ golden eagle *iolaire*
☐ greenfinch *glaisean daraich*
☐ greenshank *deoch bhuidhe*
☐ greylag goose *geadh glas*
☐ guillemot *eun dubh an sgadain*

gull
- ☐ black-headed *faoileag a'chinn dubh*
- ☐ common *faoileag*
- ☐ great black-backed *farspag*
- ☐ herring *faoileag an sgadain*
- ☐ lesser black-backed *farspag bheag*

☐ hen-harrier *breid air toin, clamhan luch*
☐ heron *corre-ghritheach*
☐ hooded crow *feannag*
☐ house sparrow *gealbhonn, glaisean*
☐ kestrel *clamhan ruadh*
☐ kittiwake *ruideag*
☐ lapwing *curracag*
☐ mallard *lach*
☐ manx shearwater *fachach*
☐ merlin *meirneal*
☐ moorhen *cearc uisge*
☐ oystercatcher *gille-bridean, trilleachan*
☐ peregrine *seabhag-gorm*

pipit
- ☐ meadow *mioneun, snathag, pipig*
- ☐ rock *gabhagan, glas-eun*

☐ pied wagtail *breac-an-sil*

plover
- ☐ golden *feadag*
- ☐ ringed *bothag*

☐ puffin *budhaig, fachach*
☐ raven *fitheag*
☐ razorbill *làmhaidh*
☐ red grouse *cearc-fhraoich*
☐ red-breasted merganser *siolta-dhearg*
☐ red-throated diver *learga-chaol*
☐ redshank *maor-cladaich, bodatha, cam-glas*
☐ redwing *deargan-sneachda*
☐ robin *brù-dearg*
☐ rockdove *calman-creige*

sandpiper
- ☐ common *luatharan, fidhleir-bord-an-lòcha*
- ☐ purple *luatharan gorm*

☐ shag *sgarbh beag*
☐ shelduck *cra-gheadh*
☐ short-eared owl *comhachag-chluasach*
☐ shoveler *gob-leathann*

skua *sasgadair*
- ☐ great (bonxie)
- ☐ arctic

☐ skylark *uiseag*
☐ snipe *naosg, gobhar-adhair*
☐ song thrush *smeòrach*
☐ starling *druid*
☐ storm petrel *annlag, luaireag*
☐ stonechat *clacharan*
☐ swallow *gobhlan gaoithe*

swan
- ☐ mute *eala-bhàn*
- ☐ whooper *eala*

tern *stearnag*
- ☐ arctic
- ☐ common
- ☐ little

☐ turnstone *trilleachan beag*
☐ tufted duck *lach-sgumanach*
☐ twite *gealan beinne*
☐ wheatear *clacharan, brù-gheal*
☐ whimbrel *guilbneach-bhealltuin*
☐ willow warbler *crionag-ghiuthais*
☐ wren *dreathan-donn*

The Scottish Wildlife Trust and Wildlife Watch

- The **Scottish Wildlife Trust** is the leading voluntary organisation for the conservation of all forms of wildlife and their habitats in Scotland.
- **SWT** manages more than 100 reserves covering some of Scotland's finest countryside.
- **SWT**'s work is supported by 15,000 members, with active branches and volunteer groups throughout Scotland.
- **SWT** works in partnership with local authorities, local enterprise companies, government agencies, private business and industry to secure the best possible future for Scotland's wildlife.
- **SWT** is committed to excellence in its active programme of conservation projects, training and environmental education.

If you would like information about membership, contact the
Scottish Wildlife Trust
Cramond House
Cramond Glebe Road
Edinburgh EH4 6NS
Tel 0131 312 7765

The Western Isles Discovery Book was written by Alison Johnson, with illustrations by Bill Neill. It was designed and typeset by the White Horse Press, Isle of Harris, and printed by Watkiss Studios, Biggleswade.

ISBN 0-9818878-5-8

The Scottish Wildlife Trust gratefully acknowledges the support of BP in Scotland and Scottish Natural Heritage.

Wildlife Watch is THE wildlife and environment club for young people and is the junior wing of the Wildlife Trusts. **Wildlife Watch** has groups across the UK, and involves thousands of young people in exciting investigations about their environment. In the past, these have included national surveys of butterflies, bees and owls, monitoring acid rain and low-level ozone pollution, and checking on the plants and animals which depend on our rivers.

All members of **Wildlife Watch** receive a full colour magazine, **Watchword**, three times a year.

To find out more, write to **Wildlife Watch** at

The Green
Witham Park,
Waterside South
Lincoln LN5 7JR

Scottish Wildlife Watch is the Scottish branch of the club, for all young Scots who care about wildlife and the environment. As a member, you have the chance to take part in local environmental investigations, surveys, activities and events. **Scottish Wildlife Watch News** brings you information about what is happening in your area.

The **Wildlife Watch Education Service** offers a unique combination of investigations, projects and games to help children enjoy, understand and monitor their local environment. Produced by **Wildlife Watch**, the materials are suitable for use in the classroom, or as the basis for informal clubs run through local youth groups, country parks or schools

The STARTER PACK for new member groups includes:-

- an **Enviroscope** action pack with 26 surveys to carry out in your local area
- ideas for developing school grounds to encourage wildlife
- Wildlife Trust contacts – giving you access to expert knowledge about local wildlife, and help with organising field visits

Regular MAILINGS include the national and **Scottish Willdlife Watch** publications above, and

- **LINK**, a photocopiable bulletin of activity ideas
- **SCOTTISH WILDLIFE**, magazine of the Scottish Wildlife Trust, to keep you up to date with conservation issues in Scotland

To find out how to join **Scottish Wildlife Watch,** or to subscribe to the **Watch Education Service,** contact SWT at the address above.